Baking
Bread
with
Kids

Jennifer Latham

Foreword by Chad Robertson

Baking Bread with Kids

Trusty Recipes for Magical Homemade Bread

Photography by Alanna Hale

Illustrations by Hennie Haworth

TEN SPEED PRESS

California | New York

Contents

Foreword by Chad Robertson

While there are many ground rules when learning to make bread, one of the most valuable keys to success is to approach the endeavor with the open and curious nature of a childlike mind. The first thing we teach new bakers at Tartine is that the process of learning never ends. By that, we mean there are always new things to learn and ways to improve. Slight adjustments in timing and techniques along the way continually lead to new discoveries for both the novice and expert baker. And when I really dig into that vague maxim—learning never ends—an extraordinary and simple truth emerges: children—young people—may be the best suited of us all to learn to make great bread.

I grew up in Texas in the '80s and tasted my first loaf of long-fermented sourdough bread as a young, but grown, man. It was truly a revelation and set the course of my life for the next several decades. In the United States, we have some bread traditions and dogmas, but nothing as old and deeply rooted as we find in many other parts of the world that have thousands of years of bread history. Early on, I became a student of these ancient traditions, but having grown up with no formal bread culture, my mind was, and is still, open and searching, looking for new ways to achieve flavors and textures. Jen lead this journey with me, managing our bread program for over a decade while helping us expand our efforts further into Los Angeles and Seoul, South Korea.

Jen and I started working together in our beloved sister restaurant, Bar Tartine, a few blocks from the original Tartine bakery. That era of Bar Tartine had a famously creative and groundbreaking chef team leading the vision at the time, and I added a small bread oven in the space to build a daytime bakery business to complement the work being done at dinner. The chef teams were there all the time, managing hundreds of ongoing fermentation projects, so why not open all day and add some bread into the mix?

Jen, it turned out, is an exceptional teacher—patient, thoughtful, dedicated, thorough, and perhaps most of all, intrepid. She has taught scores of bakers how to make great bread and to keep an open, curious mind while doing so. During the last couple of years, with young twins at home much of the time (and while writing, recipe testing, and developing for the "adult" *Bread Book* we created together), she began to teach her kids to make bread, pizza, buns, pasta, tortillas, and other bread-related foods. These recipes all have a few things in common: using long, natural sourdough fermentation and fresh-milled whole grain and high extraction flours, with a focus on making these grain-based staple foods—many of which make up a large part of American kids' daily diets—more flavorful and nutritious.

This made lots of sense once I got to know Jen, who it turns out had already tackled teaching kids a fairly complex and long-fermented game of strategy called chess while she was in college. The temperament of a chess teacher, especially one teaching grade school kids, couldn't be more well suited to teaching the strategy and approach leading to bread success. Much like making bread, lots of chess moves are carefully considered. Every action has an effect that shapes the outcome over time. To the novice, chess often has an air of mystery, as so much of the game is happening in the mind. Making bread, while having a similar air of mystery for most of us, is a much simpler undertaking. Simpler for certain, but requiring no less careful consideration as you move through the process.

Once you understand the players and tools, the universe of bread—where the sun and planets and stars are and how they move in relation to each other—you are prepared to set out on your bread-making journey. With this book, Jen is literally educating and empowering kids of current (and future) generations with knowledge we didn't gain until grown and after years of traveling to learn new perspectives from different baking traditions around the world.

For most of my life, bread was a cheap placeholder on our tables, a free basket of empty carbs and butter to fill our bellies. Over the last several years though, we've seen grain- and plant-based foods take center stage. With this lovingly crafted guidebook from one of the best bakers and teachers in the game, the possible advances and continued innovation of fermentation and grain-based regional food systems that new generations will bring are beyond exciting to imagine.

Most importantly though, all of the foods here bring joy with their sustenance. Having learned the basics, there's no limit to where young bakers may take this story, as they embark on their own path of grain and bread exploration.

—Chad Robertson
   baker/owner of Tartine Bakery and author of *Tartine Bread*

Introduction

Baking is my jam, but I wasn't born knowing how to bake. I started, like almost every baker ever, at my mother's knee making flour messes and cracking eggs everywhere. There were countless experiments, learning opportunities, and teachers along the way that brought me to being the head baker at a world-famous bakery. Every time I baked something, whether it turned out the way I expected or not, I learned something that made me wiser for the next bake. Baking is part art, part craft, and part science. Learning to see it through all those lenses is eye-opening and rewarding. Like any discipline, all you need to do is take the first step, then the next one. Before you know it, you're traveling the long path to being an expert baker.

There were many things in my childhood that nudged me toward baking. There's an illustration that my dad made inside in the front cover of a copy of Molly Katzen's *Moosewood Cookbook* (an important cookbook of the 1970s) before he gifted it to my mom. It's of me, standing on a chair in the kitchen, surrounded by mixers, spoons, bowls, and broken eggs, baking up a mess. I was three years old when he drew this. The seeds had already been sown. My dad knew.

My mom is an excellent cook and baker. Some of my earliest memories are of whisking egg whites for a chocolate mousse pie with her. She used to hold the bowl upside down over my head to check and see if the whites were stiff enough. When we moved to Germany when I was six, she mastered the local recipe for küchen, a kind of pie-cake mash-up. When my dad missed Mexican food, she made tortillas from scratch.

When I was a little older and we had moved back to the U.S., my best friend's dad owned a bakery. I remember it as the coziest, best-smelling place of all time. The truffles and pastries in the big glass case glowed like jewels in a treasure chest. I remember hanging out there one day while he made a passion-fruit wedding cake. My friend and I, in a fit of inspiration, ran to Safeway for some frozen passion-fruit juice and cake ingredients. We figured we could just add some juice to the recipe (without adding any extra flour). We made passion-fruit cake soup. But we still ate it by the spoonful. I remember it tasting pretty good.

We lived in Germany for only a few years, but one of the biggest things I missed when we moved back was the bread. Germany has some of the best bread traditions in the world. We lived in Bavaria, where sechskornbrot (six-grain bread), bauernbrot (farmer's bread), and vollkornbrot (rye bread) were on the table at almost every meal. I couldn't find anything like that when we moved back. My first real serious attempts at bread baking were to re-create those hearty, earthy, fresh breads from my childhood. I got the *Tassajara Bread Book,* written by a monk who lived in the Santa Cruz Mountains. It's a beautiful book, and its core recipe is as good a daily bread recipe as any you'll ever find. But the message—of bread baking being a never-ending path of learning—is what really sticks with me to this day and has informed so much of my baking philosophy and daily practice.

It didn't occur to me at first to bake professionally. I studied philosophy and journalism at University of California at Santa Cruz. During college I worked as a chess instructor, teaching elementary school kids. Afterward I freelanced, writing about the arts and local news for several newspapers. I moved to San Francisco, with the loose idea of becoming a writer (my lifelong dream). Meanwhile, I started working in restaurants to pay rent. I fell in love with it: the environment—the fast pace, the larger-than-life characters, the beautiful food, the friends I made—but I wasn't completely at home working in the "front of the house," greeting customers and taking orders.

The clearest aha moment happened at the kitchen table in my apartment at 17th and Dolores Streets. I was kneading bread dough (from the *Tassajara* recipe), talking to my best friend (the same one whose dad owned the bakery), and venting. I didn't want to stay a server forever, I wasn't sure how to make this writing thing work, and I didn't know what to do with my life. Go back to school? Pick a different career? What do I do? "Well, Jen," my (best-ever) friend said, nodding at the bread I was making, "some people do *that* for a living."

Be patient with your dough and yourself. Be thoughtful about your ingredients. Attention to ingredients, technique, and fermentation are the cornerstones to making good bread. Any work worth doing is worth doing carefully and correctly, without cutting any corners.

Oh. Right.

That kitchen table at 17th and Dolores in San Francisco happened to be barely two blocks away from Tartine Bakery at 18th and Guererro. It had been open at that location for about seven years. A whole lot of my writing happened at the café tables at Tartine, over coffee and a croissant, and I dreamed of being able to make that bread. I had no kitchen experience, but I started asking for a job anyway. I think I asked a dozen times over the space of a few years. I eventually got hired as a server at Bar Tartine, the sister restaurant to the bakery. I kept begging for a kitchen job until Cortney and Nick, the chefs, offered me a pastry assistant job. I did that for a year, all the while still begging to be a bread baker. Finally a spot opened up on that team and I made the cut. I was lucky to spend ten wonderful years baking bread daily at Tartine, working my way up to Director of Bread. Much of the philosophy and techniques in this book are informed and inspired by my experiences at Tartine and by my mentor, Chad Robertson.

My parents are into birds. It's their jam. Growing up, we'd hop into a fully packed car on Friday after school and drive to the Eastern Sierra, Klamath Basin, or Death Valley, chasing rare migratory birds. We'd return on Sunday night, dirty, exhausted, and exhilarated. It's both their livelihood and their passion. My brother joined in the family business, and birding is still the cornerstone of daily life for my family. They never stopped or slowed down because they had kids; they just took us with them. The thing I learned from growing up that way is that kids can do anything grown-ups can do and go anywhere grown-ups can go.

Introduction

In college, when I became a chess teacher, I learned this lesson again. Kids as young as kindergarten age can grasp complex movements and strategy if they are presented to them clearly and patiently and they are given the time and space to work out their ideas.

The cornerstone of this book is that truth: **kids can do anything they put their minds to**. Kids have the capacity for committing attention to the task. They have the patience to do things well and in their own time. Every recipe here is designed to yield exceptional results in as clear and straightforward terms as possible, because I know that kids can make exceptional bread if given the right guidance and the chance.

Baking (and baking with kids) is not for everyone, but it's a wonderfully rewarding thing to do, both on a personal level and for the spoils (warm bread). I put many of the resources, skills, recipes, tips, and perspective that I've gained in my career in this book. Bread is a lot more forgiving than people think. Even bread that doesn't turn out exactly like the picture in the book will still be utterly delicious.

I learned a lot in my years as the head bread baker at Tartine, and not just about baking. I learned a lot about learning, and it's both of those things I'm hoping to share with you in this book.

A Note on Weights and Measures

All flours, butter, eggs, salt, and other ingredients vary a little bit in composition and the weight-to-volume ratio. I've done my best to keep these recipes consistent with the most readily available products on the market, but please be mindful that there may be small variations in ingredients.

There is a tiny bit of rounding to make the metric measurements from the original baker's percentages match the closest volume measurements. If you do the baker's math from the formulas in the back, the gram measurements you get may be off by a few grams from the amounts in the recipes. The small variations in gram measurements are not enough to affect the final outcome, and the recipes as written will work just as well as the baker's percentages from the table in the back, even if they vary by a few grams here and there.

It can be tricky to get a good volume measurement for ripe sponges and starters, as the amount of gas in them (and as a result, their volume) can vary a lot. I've doubled the volume of the un-ripe sponge to get the volume of the ripe sponge for the recipes here, but for all of them, the amount of sponge you make in the recipe is the right amount for the dough (with a few grams extra, since a little will stick to the bowl). You can just put the whole thing in.

In testing these recipes, I played around with several different pan sizes. I found that one 9 by 5-inch loaf was too small an amount of dough for my mixer and two 9 by 5-inch loaves were too much. Two petite loaves, at 8½ by 4½ inches, were just the right amount of dough, and they make great kid-sized sandwiches. And we always have an extra loaf to give to a friend if we want.

Part 1

FUNDAM

Baking is a great practice in
slowness and patience.

Fundamentals for Kids

There are a few things to keep in mind as you bake that will help you be a more successful and happier baker. Take a few minutes to read through some principles of baking before starting; it will save you time and frustration during the baking process.

Plan lots of time

All of these recipes have guidelines for how much time you can expect to work on them. I estimated a little more than you might need, since everyone makes recipes at different speeds. The more you bake, the more you'll get to understand your own process and how long it will take you to do things.

There is quite a bit of downtime in bread making while you wait for doughs to ferment or proof (rise). Usually when I make bread, I also plan to do other things around the house for the day, and I go back and forth between the two. Sometimes I'll do yoga or go for a run while I'm waiting for something to bulk-ferment. Whatever it is, it's a good idea to keep yourself busy. If you don't keep busy, you'll end up staring at your dough, which seems to resist rising the more you stare at it.

How to choose what to make

If you've never baked bread before, it's a good idea to start with the simpler recipes, like honey whole wheat or focaccia. Keep the breads with the complicated shaping or long list of ingredients (like pretzels or baguettes) for later, after you've gotten comfortable with some of the easier breads. (Look for the skill level at the top of each recipe.)

Read all the way through the recipe a few times

It is very easy to miss a step or instruction the first time you read through a recipe. There is a lot of information in each one. One of the more common mistakes that even professional bakers make is that they assume they know what a recipe is going to tell them to do. Then they do what they assume instead of what is instructed. Before getting any ingredients ready, read the recipe once for an overview, then go back and read it slowly one or two more times to make sure you're not missing anything.

Imagine yourself performing the steps of the recipe

Read each step of the recipe and picture yourself doing what the instructions indicate, such as gathering the ingredients. Do you have everything you need? Is there anything to bring to room temperature (like butter or eggs) before you start?

Picture yourself mixing the ingredients. What tools will you need? Read each step carefully and think about what it will look like when you're doing it.

Think of questions that might come up and try to answer them before you get started

As you're imagining these steps, think through any questions. Maybe you're not sure if you need a mixer for this project. Maybe you're not familiar with what is meant by some of the terms, like *development* or *proofing*. If there's anything you're unsure about, there are a few things you can do. You can look the terms up in the index of this book. You also might be able to find your answers in the Key Terms (page 157) or the recommended equipment (page 28) or Troubleshooting (page 44). If you can't find answers to your questions in this book, you can try another baking book or you can do research online. You can also enlist the help of a friend or an adult assistant. It's a lot

Stages

Mixing

1. Combine wet and dry ingredients

2. Squeeze and pinch until dough comes together

3. Stretch and fold well to develop a strong, elastic dough

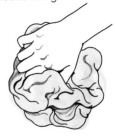

Shaping

1. Scoop the dough out of the bowl and divide it

2. Pat out dough

3. Roll up dough

4. Pinch the seam shut

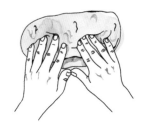

Baking

1. Brush the top of the loaf with milk

2. Snip and/or score

easier to get things cleared up before you start baking, rather than trying to search the internet with dough on your fingers.

Set up your work space

Once you've chosen your recipe and read it a few times, it's time to start gathering the things you'll need. In professional kitchens, this is often called *mise en place* (pronounced meez-ahn-plahss), a French term meaning "everything in its place." Make sure you have an open, tidy space to work in. Gather all the ingredients you'll need. Gather your equipment, including clean linens or dish towels and a hand towel.

Try to keep everything clean and tidy as you go. Take your time, move deliberately and with intention, and tidy up your last step before moving onto the next. Washing dishes and putting ingredients away as you go will make your final cleanup much easier.

Go back and read the recipe one last time, *after* you've mixed it.

Look at the amount and name of each ingredient and picture yourself adding it. Did you get all three eggs in? Did you put in 1 *teaspoon* or 1 *tablespoon* of salt? Take a moment to go back through and make sure you've added everything. At this point (for most doughs), it's not too hard to add the salt if you've forgotten it, but if you've already shaped and proofed a loaf, it's too late to add anything without deflating the dough and ruining the loaf.

Troubleshooting

At some point something will go wrong. That happens! No one and nothing is perfect, and that's more than okay.

Everyone makes mistakes—the thing that matters is how you handle them.

Listen to the little voice in your head. If it says, "This doesn't seem quite right," pause and take a step back. Take another look at your instructions. Go back through the steps you've just performed. If something seems much too wet or much too dry, there's probably something off. If you think very carefully about what you've been doing, you can often figure it out. Sometimes you won't be able to. In that case, you can try to fix it by adding more of whatever seems missing or keep going with what you have to see what happens. Either way, **embrace the learning experience that is making a mistake.**

It's easy to get flustered or overwhelmed while baking. There is a lot going on, and things can seem delicate and elaborate. If you become flustered or confused, just stop what you're doing and take a deep breath and a step back. Reread the instructions or get some help to get yourself back on track. Remember, it's just bread.

Fundamentals for Adult Assistants

Plan lots of time

The first important point for adults is the same as the first point for kids: make sure you give yourself plenty of time. Bread can be rushed, but not good bread. The slower and more patient you are with it, the better it will be. I've tried to give very generous estimates for time in this book. Bread baking is something that usually stretches out over the better part of a day, and it's a good idea to plot your schedule that way. The hands-on time is only a small fraction of the total time, though. In general, you can start your dough early in the day, tend to it occasionally (folding it or shaping it) through the middle of the day, and then bake it in the late afternoon in time for dinner. During the times when you're waiting for the dough to ferment or rise, you can do other projects like gardening, getting some chores done, exercising, running a quick errand, or just relaxing and reading a good book. If you don't have all day and need something that you can mix and bake within a couple of hours, you're better off making a cake or a quick bread. Making bread is a slow process, and that's one of the lovely things about it.

Keep expectations tempered

Bread is a practice of limitless possibilities, but that also means that there are many ways for it to go sideways, a little or a lot. The images in this book show breads made by a baker (me) who has been baking more or less daily for many years. If your breads don't look exactly like

mine, don't get discouraged, and especially don't let kids get discouraged. Focus on what was good about it—maybe it's a little wobbly on top, but it tastes wonderful. Maybe it didn't rise the way you wanted it to, but the bread will make lovely little toasts. Maybe it got baked a little dark on one side, but you can trim that off. Try doing the same recipe a few times and focus on how it improves each time. I've made sourdough bread thousands of times, and I'm still always excited to do it again and try to make it just a little better.

Hang back and let them try it, even if you don't think they're doing it "right"

It can be really, really hard to let kids try something for themselves. It's almost impossible to sit on your hands and watch someone else do something slowly and clumsily that you know you can do quickly and well, even if that someone is a quarter of your age. But if you can manage it, the rewards are exponential—watching the rush of pride and empowerment come over someone's face when they see what they've achieved with their own hands is one of life's indescribable joys. Plus, bit by bit, as kids gain confidence, dexterity, persistence, patience, and capability with "little" things like shaping a bun, those new superpowers will spill over into bigger, nonbaking achievements in their own surprising and rewarding ways.

Embrace the mess

Getting messy can be liberating, and cleaning up can be a source of calm and reward. Kids are going to get flour as well as whatever other ingredients come into play everywhere (flour, in particular, just seems designed to fly all over the place). Let them. Instead of trying to prevent the mess, let it happen and be part of the fun. If they are too focused on working cleanly, it can be discouraging and distracting. Just tidy up before moving on so that the mess doesn't accumulate. Let tidying up just be a part of the process instead of a dreaded chore. If you don't

dread it, they won't. Big cleanups can be turned into a dance party—put some music on and twirl around with a mop. One of my favorite things is to notice how great it looks when it's all cleaned up. Taking a moment to notice it together will make a clean kitchen a shared source of pleasure and pride.

Enjoy revisiting the basic mechanics of baking

Something I say over and over is that one of my favorite things about baking is that the learning process never ends. A baker is a student for life. There are simply too many recipes, too many methods, too many variables to ever be done learning it. Sometimes you will remember a forgotten early epiphany or learn something new yourself through the process of slowly and carefully enumerating each step. It's amazing how much a teacher can learn through the process of teaching. It's always a good experience to leave your own assumptions at the door and be open to learning—sometimes the teacher can even learn a thing or two from the student.

Troubleshooting

At some point in any project, things will become difficult or go wrong. That's absolutely inevitable and actually a healthy part of the learning process. It can be hard to keep that in mind in the moment, though—it is easier to get disgruntled. If a baker you know gets tired or frustrated, encourage them calmly to keep trying—being able to work through frustration is a wonderful skill. Try to encourage them to take a deep breath and think or talk through what is going on. See if it's something that can be solved: Does the dough seem too wet? Are you sure you measured everything correctly? Did you include each ingredient? I always stop myself right at the point of mixing everything and go back through each of my ingredients to make sure it's all in there and all in the right amounts, even if it's something I've done hundreds or even thousands of times. I picture myself measuring and including each thing. It's amazing how many times I've caught small errors that way—using teaspoons instead of tablespoons, forgetting the butter, picking up the baking powder instead of baking soda—in time to fix it. There have also been times I've given up on a dough I couldn't save, and that's okay, too.

Baking Science

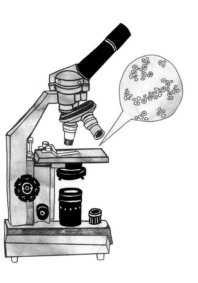

You don't *need* to know any of this stuff to bake good bread, but it really helps. The more you understand what is going on when you are mixing, shaping, and baking, the more you're able to make small adjustments and troubleshoot when things aren't going the way you expected them to.

Leavening and Fermentation

To leaven a dough means to cause it to become filled with trapped bubbles so it increases in size and volume. Examples of leavened doughs are a fluffy sandwich loaf, a bubbly focaccia, or a cake whose batter rises in the oven. Any dough that becomes larger in the oven is leavened. Examples of unleavened doughs are most crackers, matzo, and some flatbreads.

You can think of leavening as creating a foam. When you mix flour and water together, you create a solid mass. When you add a leavening agent, such as baking soda or yeast, you turn that solid mass into a foam by introducing bubbles of gas. When you bake the foam, you're setting it. A loaf of bread is just a piece of solid foam.

There are two ways to leaven a dough.

The first is to add a "chemical leavening" such as baking soda or baking powder. Baking soda and baking powder are both made with sodium bicarbonate. When sodium bicarbonate reacts with an acid, it creates carbon dioxide gas. When bubbles of this gas become trapped in dough, they create the open, fluffy crumb structure that we like in bread or cake. The difference between baking powder and baking soda is that baking powder has an acid in it (usually cream of tartar, or tartaric acid), and baking soda is only sodium bicarbonate and needs acid in the dough to react with.

Fundamentals

The second way to leaven a dough is through fermentation. Fermentation is the breakdown of a chemical substance from more complex into simpler parts through microscopic biological processes. In bread fermentation, yeast and bacteria consume the starches that are released when you create a dough of flour and water and break them down into simple sugars, acids, and gases that become trapped in the gluten network (more about gluten at right). The acids help condition the dough and give it the "sour" in sourdough.

What is gluten and how does it work?

Gluten is a protein that is unique to wheat, barley, rye, and triticale. Gluten is formed from two other proteins, glutenin and gliadin. When water is added to flour, glutenin and gliadin bond with each other (grab onto each other) and form gluten. As the dough is agitated, more gluten molecules grab on to each other. At first, the bonds are haphazard and disorganized. As dough is kneaded, the gluten molecules align and form stronger, more organized bonds. This is why the dough become stronger and stretchier as you knead it.

Gluten is a cool and unique protein. Without its distinct properties of being stretchy and strong, we wouldn't have bread as we know it.

Different grains and flours have different amounts of gluten. This is often shown as a protein percentage or labeled "high" or "low" protein. Bread flour is a high protein flour, usually 12 to 13 percent. Pastry flour is a low protein flour, usually 8 to 10 percent. All-purpose flour is in between, usually around 11 percent. These may seem like small variations, but they make a big difference in how a dough acts or how "strong" it feels. These variations can be due to different kinds of wheat that go into the flour, but they can also be affected by the conditions under which the wheat is grown, like how hot the weather is, how much water the grain gets, and

how many nutrients are available in (or added to) the soil.

On top of that, different flours can also have different combinations of glutenin and gliadin. Glutenin has more plasticity, like modeling clay. Gliadin has more extensibility, or stretchiness. Some flours, like spelt, have more gliadin. Spelt doughs will feel much more "loose," "relaxed," or "stretchy" even though they have a good amount of gluten. This variation in grains is one of the cool things that makes bread making such an endless journey of learning.

All together, the unique properties of wheat make the perfect conditions for bread. The easily fermentable starches are great food for yeast and bacteria, and the strong, stretchy gluten allows those fermentation bubbles to become trapped and make a light, fluffy loaf. **The job of the baker is to set up and gently guide this process, moving the dough along to the next steps at the right time.**

Grains and Flour

Flour is the main ingredient in most baked goods. But what is it? Flour is a substance made by grinding a grain or other dried, starchy plant matter into a powder. In the modern Western world, flour is usually made from wheat and sometimes rice, rye, or corn. Worldwide, though, there are lots of other kinds. Flour can also be made from cassava (a South American tuber that tapioca is made from), breadfruit (the starchy fruit of a tropical tree), teff (a tiny cereal grain from North Africa), chickpeas, oats, buckwheat, amaranth, almonds, and many others.

Wheat

Wheat has been grown by humans for food since the very beginnings of agriculture and civilization. Wheat is a cereal grain in the grass family. There are many, many different types of wheat, but they all belong to the same genus, *Triticum*.

The part of the wheat plant that flour is made from is the seed, sometimes called the "wheat berry." A wheat berry is made up of three main parts: the bran, the endosperm, and the germ. The bran is the outer hull that protects the inside of the seed. The endosperm is the food for the germ to consume as it turns into a plant; it serves a similar purpose that egg white serves to an unhatched chicken. The germ is the embryo of a new wheat plant, almost like the yolk of an egg.

The endosperm makes up about 83 percent of the weight of a wheat berry. It contains mostly protein and carbohydrates, as well as some fiber, minerals, and vitamins. The bran is made up mostly of fiber and contains lots of minerals and B vitamins. The germ also contains a little bit of protein and a lot of minerals and vitamins, as well as some essential fatty acids and polyunsaturated fats (the healthy kind).

Turning Wheat into Flour

Wheat berries can be cooked and eaten whole, but when they are raw and ground into flour, they become a very fermentable, more easily digestible base for many different types of foods.

Most modern commercial wheat flour is made using a roller mill. A roller mill has multiple cylinders placed parallel and close together. They roll against each other as wheat berries are fed into them. The berries are then crushed.

Stone mills were the most common type of mill for most of the history of flour. Stone mills use two disk-shaped stones stacked on top of each other, very close together. The top stone rotates and the bottom stone stays stationary. The wheat berries are fed in between them while the top one is in motion, which crushes the

Fundamentals

wheat berries into flour. Stone mills can be very large or small enough to fit on a countertop. Historically the large ones were powered by water, by wind, by horses (or other draft animals), or by hand.

Hammer mills are the third kind of mill. They work similarly to a mortar and pestle, which was probably the very earliest way that wheat berries were ground into flour. A hammer mill is made up of a hammer and a plate or shallow bowl. The berries are placed in the bowl and pounded into a powder. This type of mill is not very common anymore, as it is less efficient and effective than roller or stone mills.

Sifting is the process of removing the bran and germ to create white flour. If you've sifted flour at home in a hand sifter, you have the general idea. The flour is forced through a fine mesh, and the smallest parts, the endosperm, are separated from the larger pieces of bran and germ.

True whole wheat flours contain all of the parts of the wheat berry—the bran, the germ, and the endosperm. White flour, such as flours labeled "all-purpose flour," "bread flour," or "pastry flour," has the bran and germ removed through sifting. Because of the oils contained in the germ, even most flour labeled as "whole wheat" has some of the germ removed. The oils will cause the flour to go rancid, so it does not have the same shelf life as sifted flour. True whole wheat flour should be refrigerated if you're not using it within a few weeks.

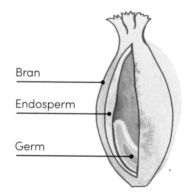

Bran

Endosperm

Germ

Steps of Bread Making

Choosing a bread to make. Choose something that you're excited about making and eating, but also something that fits your time frame and skill level (look for the skill level at the top of each recipe).

Gathering tools and ingredients. One of the most important parts is getting yourself set up. You'll want to make sure that your work space is clean and that all the tools and ingredients you're going to need are at hand.

Setting the pre-ferment. If the recipe calls for a sourdough leaven or a yeasted sponge, make that ahead of time. Most of the recipes in this book call for the sponge (pre-ferment) to be set about 3 hours before you want to mix your dough, although I've also included instructions for letting them ferment overnight if that's easier for you to schedule.

Pre-mixing. Breads that are lacy and open inside, such as ciabatta, sourdough, or focaccia, need to have a lot of care taken to develop the gluten. Time does a great job of that, so for some of these recipes, you'll see instructions to mix some or all of the wet and dry ingredients and then let them rest before finishing the mixing process. This is to allow the flour to absorb the wet ingredients and the gluten to start to develop slowly and gently, which will give you a more open crumb in the end. In baker's terms, the period of rest between pre-mixing and mixing is called the autolyze.

Mixing. In this phase you will incorporate all of the ingredients and begin to develop the gluten. Once the flour and water have been combined, the gluten doesn't form all at once. It takes time, mixing (agitation), and fermentation for the gluten to develop (for more on gluten formation and development, see What is gluten and how does it work? on page 21). Fermentation will do some of the work of developing the gluten for you. As a *very* general rule, the shorter the amount of fermentation, the longer the mixing needs to be. For example, if you're going to be using a lot of yeast and making a quick dough, you need to do more of the work manually, either with a mixer or kneading by hand. Recipes in this book generally use less yeast and allow the gluten to develop slowly.

Bulk fermentation. This is the period of rest during which the yeast and bacteria consume the paste of flour and water and excrete gases and acids that will raise (or leaven; see Baking Science on page 19 for more information) and flavor your dough. **Temperature has a tremendous amount of influence in this stage.** A dough that bulk-ferments in the refrigerator can take 8 to 12 hours to get the same amount of gas bubbles in it that a dough on a warm countertop does in a few hours. Even a few degrees one way or the other can make a tremendous difference in how long fermentation can take. This is why it is very important at this stage to "read," or observe, your dough instead of just using a timer. Always wait to move on until the dough has risen and shows signs of fermentation, such as gas bubbles and a yeasty smell. During this stage you'll usually give the dough a turn or two to even out the bubbles and the activity. This also helps with slow, gentle development.

Dividing. Once you're sure that the dough has risen sufficiently, it's time to divide it. You may divide it into two loaves if you're making pan loaves (like honey whole wheat, rye, or semolina bread) or hearth loaves (like sourdough) or into many small pieces (like for tortillas or rolls.) Depending on the dough, you may also do some gentle pre-shaping here (like for baguettes).

Shaping. During this phase, you'll train the dough into the final shape of whatever bread you're making. Here's where all that work developing the gluten pays off. A well-developed gluten will "remember" the shape you make in this stage and hold it all the way through baking. This part takes some practice, so go easy on yourself when you're just starting. It also has a tremendous bearing on the final look of your loaf. If your final loaf looks a little different than you expected, very often it's just a matter of trying it a few more times and practicing your shaping. Sometimes you'll make two loaves from the same dough, and they come out looking completely different. That's usually because they were shaped slightly differently. You can practice complicated shapes like challah braiding or pretzel knotting with playdough so that you feel comfortable before tackling the real thing.

Proofing. This is the final stage of fermenting the dough. You may also think of it as when the bread rises. This stage has a lot of influence on the flavor and structure of the final bread. Don't rush it—you really want to make sure that your dough is fluffy and airy here before baking.

Scoring. Scoring is the act of cutting or slashing the top of a loaf before baking. When you bake a dough, it rapidly expands in the oven, a phenomenon called "oven spring." Scoring the top of the dough allows the inside to expand fully during oven spring, giving you a softer and fluffier interior with a more open crumb.

Baking. The only real tricks with baking are making sure the bread bakes evenly (rotating it as necessary) and baking for the right amount of time so that it isn't underbaked (and gummy) or overbaked (and burned). In general, bake bread until it is golden brown. Also, use your sense of smell: well-baked bread has a very strong aroma of caramelized crust.

Tools and Equipment

Tools for Mixing

Bowls. You'll need a few different bowls for mixing. I recommend getting one big workhorse bowl for hand-mixing most doughs. It's best to get one that is made from an insulating material like glass, as opposed to metal. Metal bowls conduct heat away from the dough more effectively. This means the dough gets cooler faster, and keeping doughs warm is an important part of keeping fermentation going. I also like glass bowls because you can see what is going on with your dough. One of the best indicators of fermentation is the formation of bubbles, which can be clearly seen if you have a clear glass bowl.

A few other size bowls are handy, too. Some recipes will have you mix wet ingredients and dry ingredients separately and then combine the two or weigh something separately before adding. An assortment of small, medium, and large bowls will come in handy.

Hands. This may seem like a funny thing to include in the equipment section, but your hands are one of your most important tools. A whole lot of doughs can be mixed by hand instead of with a mixer. This is convenient because you may not want to wrestle with the mixer or you may not have one available. It's also a really great way to get used to feeling the dough for strength and temperature. But it definitely gets your hands doughy and messy, and that's okay. The plastic bowl scraper mentioned below is a great tool for scraping dough off your hands and back into the bowl. It's still dough! One of the coolest things about gluten is its ability to seemingly magically heal itself—the scrapings will disappear and become bread again.

Jars. I like to use wide-mouth pint-size and quart-size mason jars for feeding pre-ferments and for storing ingredients. You could also use plastic deli containers or small bowls—all of these are equally functional. Use whatever you prefer.

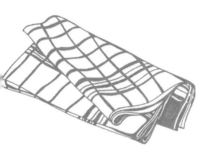

Linens. Clean linens are great for covering bowls of dough to keep them warm and to keep a skin from forming on the dough. Some of the doughs (like baguettes and ciabatta) will actually have you rest the shaped loaf in a well-floured piece of clean linen. I have a few designated linens I use just for bread, so no one else minds if they get a little crusty. Look for tightly woven linens made with natural, untreated materials such as cotton, hemp, or (my favorite) flax/linen.

Measuring cups and spoons (tiny). Even though I highly encourage using a scale (see Scale, page 30) to weigh ingredients, I've included volume measurement in this book because I understand that not everyone will have a scale or want to use one. A sturdy set of measuring cups is, undoubtably, a kitchen staple. I like the ones made from metal. Measuring spoons are especially useful. Ingredients like salt and yeast are often called for in amounts that are too small for most kitchen scales. For baking, you'll want a set with the extra tiny spoons. Look for one that has a "pinch" spoon, or 1/16 teaspoon—you'll actually use this one when making an overnight sponge.

Measuring pitcher. This is one of my indispensable tools. I keep a large Pyrex measuring bowl handy for measuring liquids into doughs, but I also use it to dampen my hands when I'm mixing and folding doughs and for cleaning my work surface.

Mixer. A countertop electric stand mixer with a removable bowl and several options for mixing attachments is very handy for quickly and efficiently combining ingredients and mixing doughs, especially wet or sticky ones. Many of the recipes in this book don't require a mixer or give you an option to use one. The few that do require a mixer, though, really need one. It's very difficult to mix the butter into brioche any other way, for example. There are several companies that make solid, reliable stand mixers. If you're interested in baking bread and pastry, they are a great investment and will open up a whole world of cakes, confections, and enriched breads. I have a KitchenAid, which has the bonus of having some great attachments like a grain mill (!) and a pasta extruder, among others.

Plastic bowl scraper. This is a flexible plastic tool that conforms to the shape of a bowl. It's very useful for cleaning the sides of the bowl and your hands when mixing. It's also useful for scooping dough out of the bowl and for dividing and shaping doughs.

Scale. A scale is an indispensable tool for a baker. Baking is notorious for being fickle, and a big part of that is because if your ingredients are out of balance, it can have a dramatic effect on how your dough feels and how your bread turns out. Measuring things accurately with cups and spoons is actually very difficult. If you scoop 1 cup of all-purpose flour out of the bag with a cup measure, you might get about 170 grams of flour. If you gently spoon sifted flour into a cup measure, you'd probably get about 120 grams of flour. That's a 70 percent difference! A 70 percent difference in flour can make the difference between a dough that is too runny and sticky to shape and bread that is gummy inside or a perfectly good, sturdy loaf. **One of the most impactful things you can do to make your baked goods more consistent is to weigh your ingredients.**

Weighing ingredients is also a little faster and cleaner. You can start with one bowl, weigh your first ingredient in, tare the scale, weigh your second ingredient, tare it again, and so forth. Instead of getting however many different size measuring cups and spoons dirty, you've just put everything straight into a bowl.

The cost of digital kitchen scales can start at very affordable and can end up very expensive. The one I use all the time at home costs $24 and has lasted me for years. It won't weigh out the very smallest amounts, but scales that weigh into

Almost all kitchen scales have a button on them that says "tare." The tare button will set the scale back to zero, regardless of what weight is already on it. In order to weigh 500 grams of flour into a bowl, for example, you can put the bowl on the scale, press *tare* to zero out the weight of the bowl, then add flour until the scale reads "500 grams." Say you want to add 10 grams of salt next. You can press *tare* again, setting the scale to zero out the weight of the bowl and the flour, then add salt until the sale reads "10 grams." Pretty nifty stuff.

the fractions of grams (useful for very tiny amounts of yeast) are also available for a very affordable price. At Tartine, we used a large scale for huge amounts of flour and a separate tiny "yeast" scale ($12) to weigh all the yeast.

Spatula. A rubber or silicone spatula is especially helpful for stickier doughs or doughs that go in the mixer, like brioche and rolls. It's not an essential tool for bread baking, though, and I find myself mostly using my plastic bowl scraper for the same purposes.

Spoons. Wooden spoons can be useful if you really don't want to get your hands dirty. A spoon can be used to stir a sponge or a starter. I enjoy feeling the dough in my hands, though, and I don't use these very much.

Thermometer. A small digital thermometer can be very handy for checking water and dough temperatures. It's always a good idea to feel your doughs and listen to your hands to get a sense of whether doughs are warm enough (or too warm!), but a thermometer can be a great way to double-check.

Tools for Shaping

Metal bench scraper. I feel more affection for my bench scraper than anyone really should for any kitchen thing. If I lost a hand like Captain Hook, I think I'd have it replaced with a metal bench scraper. It's just such a great all-around tool for picking up sticky doughs, rounding them nicely, and scraping worktables clean.

Pastry brush. Many of these formulas will instruct you to brush the tops of the loaves or rolls with milk, melted butter, buttermilk, or another wash. This helps the loaf to rise nicely in the oven and to get a nice crust. A simple, clean pastry brush, 1 or 1½ inches wide, will do nicely for this purpose. Make sure to clean and dry it promptly after each use, and it will last for a long time.

Tools for Baking

Baking stone or steel. A baking stone or steel serves the same purpose: it stores a lot of heat so that when dough is placed on top, there is a sustained, rapid transfer of heat from the baking surface to the dough. This creates a lot of oven spring and good browning. It's useful for any free-form loaves (loaves that are not baked in a pan, like baguettes), but it's particularly important for pizza.

Bread pan. All the recipes in this book are designed for two 8½ by 4½-inch loaf pans. The 9 by 5-inch loaf pan is also pretty standard, but there's actually a 15 percent difference, so a loaf designed for a 9 by 5-inch pan may burst out of an 8½ by 4½-inch pan, and conversely, a loaf designed for a 8½ by 4½-inch pan will be a little squat in a 9 by 5-inch pan. I like the metal and stoneware ones best, as they conduct a lot of heat to the breads and result in a nice brown crust and beautiful oven spring.

Cast-iron skillet. The focaccia and cornbread recipes give instructions to bake them in an 8-inch cast-iron skillet. While this isn't strictly necessary, it definitely gets the best results. Cast-iron skillets are kitchen workhorses and should be considered by anyone who enjoys cooking or baking.

Cooling rack. When bread comes out of the oven, it needs to finish setting and release some steam and heat. Cooling is really the final stage of baking. This works best when there is air circulation all around the loaf. I like to set it on a sheet pan–size cooling rack until it is just warm to the touch before doing anything else with it.

Oven. Most of the time, you're not going to have much choice in your oven. There is a whole lot of variation in them, though. Some heat up in 10 minutes, some take an hour. Some will actually be the temperature you set them at, and some will vary by 50°F. I like to keep a little oven thermometer in my oven so that I can get accurate information about what the real temperature is. Keep an eye on your bread as it bakes, too, and **always act on**

what is actually happening instead of what you think is supposed to happen. For instance, don't let a loaf burn just because the instructions say to leave it in for 5 more minutes. If you know your oven runs a little hot, be prepared to keep an eye on your bread and take it out a little early, or maybe set the temperature a little lower than instructed.

Peels (baguette and pizza). If you want to bake baguettes or pizza, you'll need a peel. A peel is a thin piece of wood (or sometimes metal), often with a handle, for sliding dough onto a baking surface (such as a steel or a stone) and removing it when it's done baking. It doesn't have to be fancy at all. The thinner the better. A baguette peel is simply a long, thin rectangular piece of wood that you use to pick up a raw baguette and transfer it to the oven to be baked. If you only want one peel, a pizza peel can be used for both, but baguettes are easier to bake with a baguette peel. If you don't have a peel, you can use the back of a cookie tray or a sheet pan, dusted generously with cornmeal.

Scissors or a sharp knife for scoring. You'll need to slice the top of the loaf before baking so that it can open up properly in the oven. This can be done with a small sharp knife, like a paring knife, or with a razor blade attached to a handle (bakers even have a special handle, called a lame, for this.) You can also just use a pair of sharp-tipped kitchen scissors. I have of small Japanese pruning shears I got at a garden store years ago that work wonderfully for scoring bread.

Sheet pans. Sheet pans are pretty universally useful in the kitchen, and not just for baked goods. Several of these recipes, such as for the rolls and crackers, will need to be baked on a sheet pan. In a pinch, you can also turn it over and use it as a peel.

Tools for Serving

Bread knives. A sharp serrated knife is best for cutting into crusty loaves of bread or neatly dividing buns in half. A serrated knife will last a long time but is almost impossible to sharpen. It doesn't need to be expensive or fancy to be perfectly functional.

Cutting boards. I have two kinds of cutting boards: the beat-up, heavily used ones that I cut on daily, and then one or two nice boards that I use for presentation. The latter aren't strictly necessary, but if you have a pretty one, take good care of it. Don't let it sit in water, and use food-grade mineral oil on it once in a while.

Sponges and Sourdough

Pre-ferments

Many bread recipes will instruct you to simply mix flour, water, and yeast together to make your dough (with maybe a few other ingredients). This is known as a "direct dough" in the baking world.

Alternatively, you can mix some portion of the dough ahead of time and let it ferment before mixing the rest of the dough. **Fermenting some of the dough for a longer period of time is the single biggest thing a baker can do to the improve the flavor and texture of the bread, as well as make it easier to digest.** Any portion of the dough that is fermented before you add it to the final dough is called a **pre-ferment**. A dough made with a pre-ferment is called an "indirect dough." Sourdough bread is a great example of an indirect dough. You ferment a little bit of flour and water ahead of time, then add that to rest of the ingredients during the mixing phase. In the case of sourdough, this addition of some pre-fermented flour and water is what starts the fermentation in your dough by introducing the right yeasts and bacteria.

There are many names for sourdough pre-ferments—sourdough starter, mother, natural leaven, wild leaven, or levain (from French), but they are all made with yeast and bacteria that are cultivated from the natural environment, the baker's hands, and the wheat itself. There is no instant, dry, fresh, or cake (commercial) yeast added.

Alternatively, you can also make a pre-ferment with added commercial yeast (in this case, it's not called "sourdough" since you're adding commercial yeast.) To do so, you would mix together a little bit of flour, water, and commercial yeast and let it ferment before making the dough. Sometimes this will be the only yeast you'll

add to the dough; sometimes you'll add both some pre-ferment and some commercial yeast. There are many different kinds of added-yeast pre-ferments—some are stiff and dry, some are almost liquid. There are many different names for these, too—biga, poolish, and soaker are a few. For the sake of simplicity in this book, I will use the term "sponge" to refer to any pre-ferment made with added commercial yeast.

There are several kinds of commercial yeasts available: active dry, instant dry, and fresh, or cake yeast. Active dry yeast and instant yeast are very similar. They are dehydrated (dried) yeasts, powdered and shaped into tiny pellets. The dehydration makes the yeast inactive—almost like hibernation. Once you add them to liquid, they become active again and can start fermenting. The biggest difference is that you can add instant yeast directly to a dough, and active yeast needs to be activated first, usually by mixing it with a little warm water and sugar. Fresh or cake yeast isn't dehydrated, so it's very perishable. I've specified instant here because it's the easiest to use. If you have active instead of instant, you can use it in the same amounts; just make sure you're mixing it into a liquid and let it rest for a minute before adding flour. Active can sometimes take a little longer, so if you're substituting active yeast in these recipes, make sure you give the dough all the time it needs to rise fully. Fresh yeast needs to be used in different amounts than dry yeast. I love fresh yeast, but I haven't formulated these recipes to use it.

Sponges

One of the biggest things you can do to add flavor, improve texture, and make your bread more easily digestible is to add a pre-ferment. When you add commercial yeast to a dough and ferment it quickly, you don't get much or any bacterial fermentation, so you don't create the acids that condition the dough and add flavor, and you don't break down the starches as much. This means that most direct doughs get their flavor from additions, such as butter, milk, sugar, oil, or others. Indirect doughs get more flavor from the grain itself and fermentation of that grain.

What is yeast?

Commercial yeast is yeast that has been cultivated in lab for baking use (or for brewing beer). All commercial yeast is the species *Saccharomyces cerevisiae*. This strain is particularly good at raising bread and making beer. To make the yeast you buy in grocery stores, the *Saccharomyces cerevisiae* is fed a sugar, usually molasses. After it grows and reproduces, making more yeast, it is isolated in a centrifuge (a machine that spins very fast). The result is a creamy substance made of yeast organisms, which can be sold as "fresh yeast" if kept refrigerated and used quickly. It can also be dehydrated to make a shelf-stable yeast powder, called instant dry or active dry yeast. It is rehydrated and becomes active when you add it to water and feed it flour. Fun fact: Yeasts are members if the kingdom Fungi, along with molds and mushrooms. There are more than 1,500 known species of yeast. Some of them are critical to the function of your digestive system. In fact, your body, inside and out, is actually covered with microscopic yeast cells (it's a good thing.) Yeast is also used to make some medicines and biofuels.

You will see recipes for both direct and indirect doughs in this book. I realize that you don't always know several hours or the night before you're going to make bread. You may not have the chance to mix your sponge ahead of time. I have used sponges in the recipes that I think will benefit most from them. For recipes that have other additions for flavor, I have mostly skipped it.

Many of the recipes in this book call for making the sponge 3 hours before mixing the dough. I did this so that you could get the flavor boost from having a pre-ferment in the dough but could still make bread in one day. For every recipe in this book that calls for making the sponge 3 hours before mixing the dough, you could alternatively make the sponge the night before. To do so, follow the recipe for the sponge but instead of leaving it at room temperature

for 3 hours, leave it at room temperature for 1 hour, and then put it in the refrigerator overnight. Take it out and let it come to room temperature for 1 hour before adding it to your dough.

If you're a sourdough baker and have some sourdough starter going, you can substitute a mature sourdough starter for the sponge in any recipe in this book.

If you've tried one of the direct recipes a few times and want to change it to an indirect dough, you can usually add a pinch of sponge or sourdough to your wet ingredients and reduce the commercial yeast by half or even eliminate it. The dough will take longer to rise and proof and will need to be kept warmer.

Sourdough

One of the most intimidating but rewarding skills in any baker's toolbox is knowing how to make sourdough bread. It's not as complicated as you might think—it's a lot like keeping a pet.

What is a starter? A starter is a colony of the particular strains of yeast and bacteria that will leaven and flavor sourdough bread. You can create more of these organisms by placing a small amount of culture into a fresh mixture of flour and water. The yeast and bacteria in the small amount of culture will consume the hydrated flour and reproduce, creating simple sugars, gases, and acids as well as more yeasts and bacteria. To make sourdough bread, simply add some starter to your the flour and water in the mixing phase of the recipe and keep it warm enough to ferment.

Sourdough breads start off with fewer yeast organisms than doughs with added commercial yeast. This means that it is more important to make an ideal living environment for the yeast: warm, moist, and with fresh air. It also means that sourdoughs take longer to rise and proof—anywhere from a few hours to overnight. That timeline means more time for the flavor and texture to develop.

Sourdough Starter

How to make a sourdough starter

All of the yeasts and bacteria that are needed to make bread occur naturally on your hands, on the wheat, and maybe even in your kitchen already.

To start a starter, all you need to do is mix some flour and water together and wait for it to ferment. I like to use some whole wheat flour—the bran and germ are great food for the microorganisms.

How to feed a starter

Once your starter shows signs of fermentation, it is called a "ripe" starter. This means that it is ready to be used for bread. In order to keep it healthy so that it will raise dough, you have to "feed" it once a day or so (aim for once a day, but if you miss a day, don't sweat it and just start up again the next day). If you don't give the yeast and bacteria fresh flour to consume, they will starve and die out. To feed your starter, simply follow the Feeding Your Starter recipe on page 43, adding a pinch of your ripe starter to a fresh mixture of flour and water. On days that you want to make bread, follow the instructions for making enough starter for the dough (in the recipe). On days you're not baking, follow the instructions for the Feeding Your Starter (see page 42), to keep it healthy; if you're not baking very often, you can keep your starter in the refrigerator for up to a week (see page 42), but then you'll need to feed it once or twice before baking with it to restore it to peak performance.

You'll also have some starter left over every time you take a little bit out to feed it. If you've made about a cup of starter and you take out 1 tablespoon, you still have most of that cup left over. What do you do with it? It's hard to throw it away after working so hard to cultivate it. You can

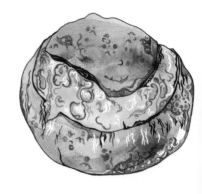

New Starter Formula

Ingredients

¼ cup (59 grams) warm
water (about 85°F)

¼ cup (35 grams)
bread flour

¼ cup (35 grams)
whole wheat flour

In a wide-mouth pint-size glass mason jar or other small, clear vessel, add the water, bread flour, and whole wheat flour. Mix well with your hand (some of the yeasts and bacteria from your hands are important for getting the starter going!) until all the ingredients are combined. Use a small plastic dough scraper or a spoon to scrape your fingers and the sides of the jar clean. Cover the jar loosely with a small piece of clean linen or a loose top (the culture needs oxygen to ferment).

Keep the jar in a warm place (but out of direct sunlight), such as on top of a turned-off stove or on a warm draft-free corner of the counter. Stir the contents with your fingers two or three times a day.

Look for signs of fermentation. These are bubbles, a sour smell, a change in volume, or liquid separating on the top of the mixture. It can take anywhere from 24 hours to 5 days to see these signs. When you notice signs of fermentation, proceed to the next section, Feeding Your Starter, page 43.

When you're starting a new starter fresh, it is best to give it a few feedings, waiting for signs of fermentation each time before feeding it again (usually between 1 and 3 days for a brand-new starter). After a few feedings, it should grow significantly. This lets you know that you have a robust culture that will reliably raise bread. A mature starter is one that has increased dramatically in volume, smells slightly sour, and contains lots of bubbles.

save it in the fridge for up to a week and use it to flavor tortillas, pasta, waffles, or brownies—basically anything that will benefit from sourdough flavor but doesn't need a very robust starter to give the dough lots of gas bubbles.

There are lots of great recipes that use discard sourdough out in the world, although I don't go into it too deeply in this book. The exception is the sourdough crackers on page 127. That's my favorite thing to do with sourdough discard. Sometimes I save my discard, but often I just compost it. If you have a garden, you can even just bury it straight in the soil—it composts very quickly and is great for the worms.

How to store starter if you're not using it regularly

Most of use aren't going to bake with sourdough every day or even every week. Once you have a starter going, sometimes you're going to want to put it to sleep until you're ready to use it again. My favorite way to do this is to dry it out and cool it down. Remember the dehydrated yeast that becomes shelf-stable (page 37)? With less hydrated flour to feed on, yeast slows down its metabolism and reproductive cycles (kind of like a hibernating bear).

To dry out your starter at home, mix ¼ cup of ripe starter with enough flour to form a very stiff dough—as stiff as you can knead. Place that in an airtight jar in the fridge. It will keep for up to 2 weeks this way. When you're ready to wake it up, use this stiff starter in the Starter Formula on page 43. It's best to feed it once or twice (for a day or two) before using it again once you've woken it up. Use the Starter Formula for these feedings.

To store starter for a very long time, spread a very thin layer of ripe starter on a sheet tray and let it dry overnight or for a day or two. (I like to leave it in a turned-off oven to keep it out of the way; it provides perfect conditions for drying.) Once it's all the way dry, that's it! You have starter flakes—instant sourdough starter. Use the flakes as you would the ripe starter in the Feeding Your Starter recipe (page 43).

Feeding Your Starter

Ingredients

¼ cup (59 grams) warm
    water (about 85°F)

¼ cup (35 grams)
    bread flour

¼ cup (35 grams)
    whole wheat flour

1 tablespoon (14 grams)
    ripe starter

This is the recipe to use once your starter is thriving. If you want to keep it in peak form but aren't using it to bake that day, feed it using this method.

In a wide-mouth pint-size mason jar, add the warm water, bread flour, whole wheat flour, and ripe starter.

Mix well with your hands until all the ingredients are combined. Use a small plastic dough scraper or a spoon to scrape your fingers and the sides of the jar clean. Cover it loosely with a small piece of clean linen or a loose top (the culture needs oxygen to ferment.)

Keep the jar in a warm, draft-free spot (but out of direct sunlight). Stir the contents with your fingers two or three times a day. Feed it every 24 hours or so, keeping it somewhere warm and stirring it once or twice between feedings.

Use this starter to feed the leaven for sourdough bread (page 144) or to ferment any leavened dough.

Troubleshooting

Problem

The bread doesn't rise in the oven, the score doesn't open, and/or the crust is wrinkly, soft, and/or chewy. These can all be signs that your dough was overproofed. What does that mean?

Overproofing means that you waited too long to divide the loaves after the rising-in-the-bowl stage (the bulk rise) or after you shaped them but before you baked them. In this situation, the yeasts have consumed all the starches, and there are none left for them to eat during the beginning of the baking stage. If the loaf is proofed just right, oven spring occurs (see Baking Science on page 19) during the beginning of baking, the loaf rises a little more, and the score opens. If there isn't any starch left to consume or any more hungry yeast, then oven spring doesn't occur and you get a flat loaf. This also can also cause the crust to be wrinkly and chewy.

How to fix it

Divide the dough and/or bake the loaves a little earlier next time. After your dough is shaped, it is ready to bake when the dough bounces back slowly when you press it with a fingertip. If the dough holds the shape of your fingertip and doesn't spring back at all, you've let it go too far.

The bread doesn't get a nice even color in the oven, the crust tears, and/or the inside is gummy. Two things could be wrong here. First, your loaf may need more time in the oven. All ovens are different, and some take longer to bake a loaf of bread than others. If you're sure you've baked the loaf long enough and it's still not turning a nice, even medium brown, there might be something else going on. All of these can also happen if you underproof your dough. What does that mean?

It means you haven't waited for the dough to rise enough during the bulk rise in the bowl and/or after you shaped it and before you baked it. If you haven't let it rise enough, a few things will go wrong. Remember in the Baking Science section (page 19), when we talked about the yeast eating the starches in the dough and turning them into sugars? Sugar is what browns in the oven during baking. If you don't have enough starch turned into sugar, the loaf won't turn brown.

Also, if those yeasts haven't eaten through much of the starch yet, there will still be lots of starch for them to eat, and when you put your loaf in the oven, all the slow rising that didn't occur during the proofing stages happens all at once and the crust will tear during the explosive feeding frenzy.

One last thing that happens during the rising stage is that the gluten forms— that's the web of protein that gives your dough strength. If you cut that short, the gluten doesn't form all the way, and the interior of the loaf will be gummy.

How to fix it

Let the dough rise longer next time. Make sure that it doubles in size in the bowl and you see lots of bubbles. After it is shaped, don't bake it until you see it rise significantly again. It should feel very fluffy and airy and spring back slowly when you gently poke it with a fingertip.

Part 2

REC

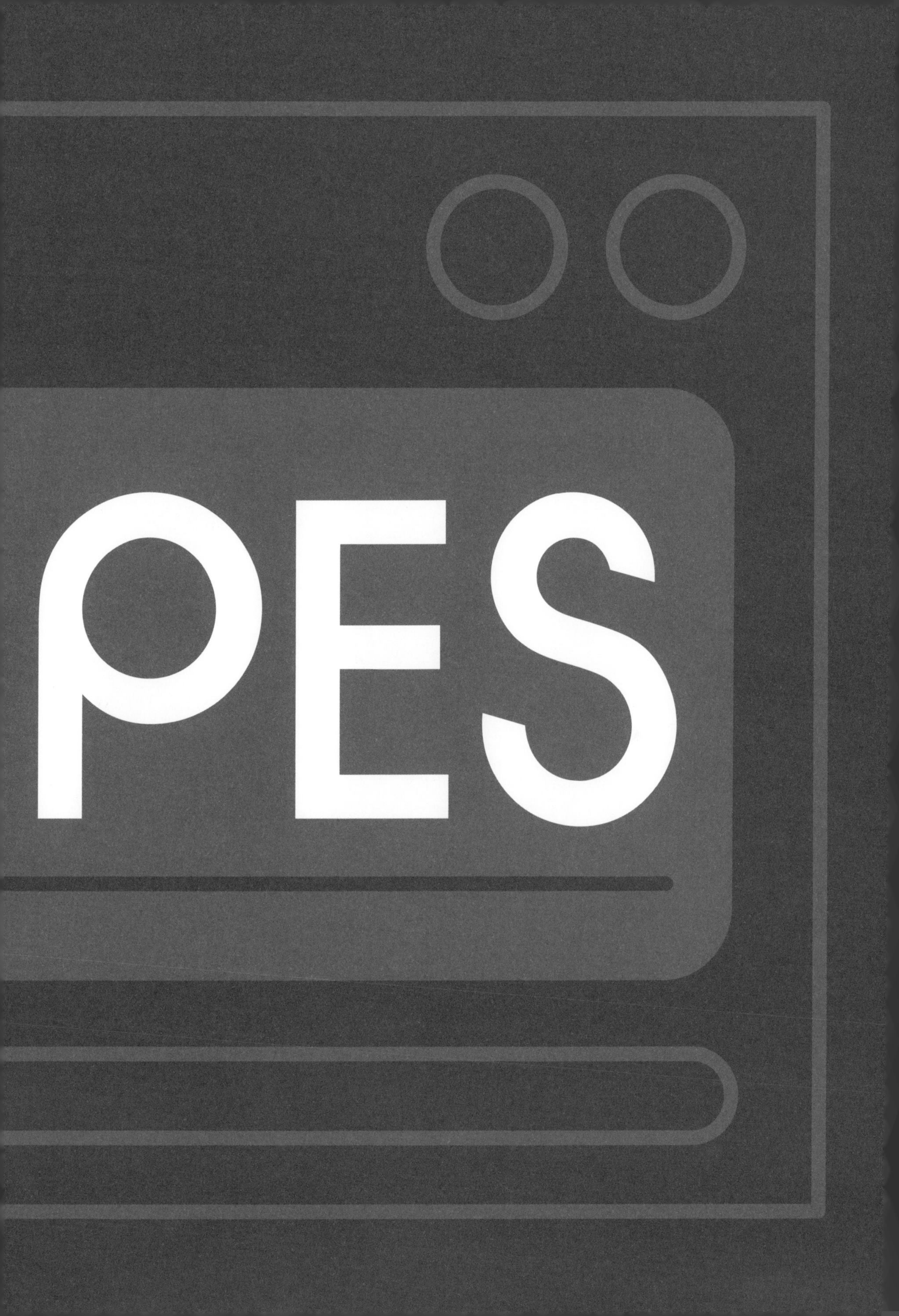
PES

Honey Whole Wheat Bread

Makes Two 8½ by 4½-inch loaves

Difficulty level Beginner

Time from start of mixing to baked bread 6 hours (plus 3 hours ahead to prepare the sponge)

Baking vessel Two 8½ by 4½-inch bread pans

Mixer Optional

This is a great bread recipe to make if you've never made bread before. It has all the building blocks that you'll need to make any dough: mixing, fermenting, dividing, shaping, and baking. The ingredients are uncomplicated—just flour, water, sponge, honey, yeast, and salt. The whole wheat flour in the recipe makes it both delicious and healthy. (For more on whole wheat flour, see Turning Wheat into Flour on page 23). This means you can make it a lot and eat it as a staple part of a balanced diet. The more often you bake it, the more familiar you become with it. With practice, you'll start to be able to tell more easily when it's ready to divide or bake. When you have gotten comfortable and familiar with all the steps, you're on your way to becoming a master bread baker.

The first bread I became obsessed with making myself was a honey whole wheat bread. To this day, the smell of the wheat flour, honey, and yeast transports me to all the places I have mixed this bread: on my mother's kitchen counter, at my best friend's house after school, on the thrift store table in my college apartment, in the first kitchen I shared with my now-husband. Making this bread is as comforting to me as eating it is.

In one of my favorite baking books, *The Tassajara Bread Book*, the author Edward Espe Brown says, "Bread makes itself by your kindness, with your help, with imagination streaming through you, with dough under your hand, you are breadmaking itself, which is why breadmaking is so fulfilling and rewarding." Making this bread reminds of that quote every time.

Continued ∿

Ingredients

Sponge
(make 3 hours ahead)

1 cup (236 grams) warm
  water (about 85°F)

½ teaspoon (2 grams)
  instant dry yeast

1 cup (140 grams)
  bread flour

1 cup (140 grams)
  whole wheat flour

Dough

1⅔ cups (393 grams) warm
  water (about 85°F)

1 tablespoon + 2 teaspoons
  (35 grams) honey

6 cups (481 grams) sponge

1 teaspoon (4 grams) instant
  dry yeast

1 tablespoon + 1 teaspoon
  (12 grams) kosher salt

1¾ cups (245 grams)
  whole wheat flour

1¾ cups (245 grams)
  bread flour

2 tablespoons unsalted
  butter, room temperature
  (or neutral oil), for
  greasing the pans

2 tablespoons olive oil,
  for brushing the top of
  the loaf before baking

To make the sponge

Measure the water into a medium mixing bowl—make sure there is plenty of room for the sponge to grow. Sprinkle the yeast on top of the water, then stir to dissolve the yeast. Add both flours to the bowl, stirring until well combined and there are no lumps. Cover the mixing bowl with a clean linen and let rest on the countertop in a warm, draft-free spot for 3 hours. It's ready to use when it has doubled in size and is very bubbly.

To make the dough

In a large mixing bowl, combine the warm water, honey, sponge, and yeast. Stir with your hand or a wooden spoon to combine (the sponge doesn't need to dissolve completely, just be broken up a bit). Add the salt and stir to dissolve.

Add the whole wheat and the bread flours to the wet ingredients in the bowl and stir until there is no more dry flour. Let the dough rest for 3 minutes so the flour can begin to absorb the water and the gluten can start to form.

After 3 minutes, wet your hand and mix the dough well in the bowl for about 5 minutes, squeezing to make sure everything is well combined, and then lifting, stretching, folding, and pressing it down. Mix in this way until the dough is smooth, stretchy, and strong. It should still feel a little bit sticky. Alternatively, mix the dough in the bowl of a stand mixer fitted with the dough hook on low for about 5 minutes.

Scrape any dough off your fingers and the edges of the bowl back onto the dough—it will heal itself like magic and become part of the dough again!

Shaping

1. Scoop the dough out of the bowl and divide it

2. Pat out dough

3. Roll up dough

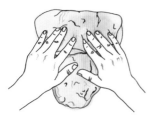

4. Pinch the seam shut

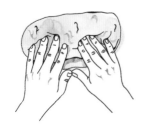

Cover the bowl with a clean linen and place in a warm, draft-free spot to rise Let it rest for 30 minutes to allow the gluten to relax.

After 30 minutes, fold the dough. This will even out the temperature, re-distribute areas of more activity, and strengthen the gluten. To do so, loosen it from the edges of the bowl. Lift the side of the dough up, stretch it over the top, and press it back down into the bowl. Do this a few times until you have lifted, stretched, and folded all the dough.

Cover it again and let it rest for 30 minutes.

After 30 minutes, fold the dough one more time.

Cover it again and let it rest for 30 minutes to 1 hour. After this last rest, it should have risen noticeably in the bowl. You should be able to see bubbles at the edges or top of the dough. If you can see the rising and the bubbles, it's time to divide the dough. If not, let it rest for 15 more minutes. Check the dough every 10 to 15 minutes and divide it when you see a dramatic increase in size and lots of bubbles.

While it's finishing rising in the bowl, get two 8½ by 4½-inch rectangular bread pans ready by lightly buttering the sides. Use your fingers or a pastry brush to spread the soft butter evenly all over the inside of the pans. Alternatively, brush them with neutral oil.

To divide the dough, scoop it out of the bowl (a bowl scraper is handy for this, but you can also use a spatula or just your fingers). Divide the dough equally in half using your bench knife to gently cut it. If you are using a scale, each half should weigh about 700 grams.

To shape the loaves, pat each portion of the dough gently into a rectangle, roughly 12 by 6 inches. The shorter sides of the rectangle should be at the top and bottom, and the longer sides should be on the right and left sides. Shape one loaf at a time. Using your fingertips, roll the top edge

Continued ∿

Baking

1. Brush the top of the loaf with olive oil

2. Snip and/or score

toward you, almost as if you're rolling up a carpet. Press the rolled part gently into the flat part as you continue to roll it toward you. Once it's all rolled up, press the seam together where the bottom edge meets the rolled-up part of the loaf. Place the shaped loaf into the pan with the seam on the bottom. Repeat with the second loaf.

Preheat the oven to 400°F and place a rack in the middle position (get an adult assistant to help if needed).

Let the loaves rise for 30 minutes to an hour, until they have risen taller than the loaf pans. If you poke a loaf gently with your fingertips, they should feel full of air and spring back slowly. Wait until they have risen noticeably in the pan before you bake them, even if it takes more than an hour. Once they have risen in the pan (the final proofing), you're ready to bake.

Using a clean pastry brush, brush the tops of the loaves with olive oil so that they are evenly coated.

Next, score the loaves (for more about scoring, see page 159). Use some sharp kitchen scissors to snip the top six to eight times (get an adult assistant to help if needed). Alternatively, use a sharp knife to make small slits or slashes in the top of each loaf.

Once the loaves have been brushed with olive oil and scored, you are ready to put them in the oven. Place the pans gently on the rack in the middle of the oven (get an adult assistant to help if needed). Close the oven door and set a timer for 20 minutes.

After 20 minutes, take a peek at your loaves. If it looks like either is darker on one side, use oven mitts to turn the pans half a turn so that they will finish baking evenly (get an adult assistant to help if needed).

Bake for 10 to 15 more minutes. The loaves are finished baking when they are an even medium brown all over the top. If they look speckled or blonde, give them a few more minutes. Remember, your oven may run a little hot. If they are well browned on top, go ahead and take them out.

When they are done baking, use oven mitts to remove the pans from the oven (get an adult assistant to help if needed). Set the pans on a heatproof surface (such as a stovetop) to cool for 10 minutes.

After 10 minutes, gently remove the loaves from the pans (get an adult assistant to help if needed). Set each loaf on a cooling rack and let cool for at least 1 hour.

You can keep your bread in a bread box or bag on the countertop for up to 4 days. If it starts to feel stale, you can cut slices and toast them. To store it for longer, slice it and keep it in a sealed container in the freezer. To serve, take as many slices as you'd like from the freezer and toast them.

Variation
Seeded Honey Whole Wheat Bread

Preheat the oven to 350°F. About 30 minutes before you begin mixing your dough, weigh out ⅓ cup (50 grams) of sesame seeds, ⅓ cup (50 grams) of sunflower seeds, and ⅓ cup (50 grams) of pumpkin seeds. Mix them together and spread them evenly on a sheet pan. Toast them in the oven for 7 to 10 minutes, until they are fragrant and starting to lightly brown. Set them aside and let them cool. When you are adding the flour to your water mixture, mix the toasted seeds in also. After the loaf has proofed, brush it with water and sprinkle with some raw (untoasted) seeds on top before scoring and baking.

Homemade Butter

Makes 1 cup butter and 1 cup buttermilk

Ingredients

1 pint heavy cream, fresh and very cold

1 quart-size wide-mouth mason jar

A fine-mesh strainer

What's more perfect with fresh bread than fresh butter? It's easy and fun to make butter at home yourself. You also get buttermilk! The buttermilk can be saved for other recipes, like biscuits or cake, or you can simply dip your bread in it—it's delicious!

This is a great activity to do while you're waiting for your bread to bake. When you're done, you'll have fresh bread and butter.

Put the very cold cream into a wide-mouth pint-size mason jar and close the lid very tightly (you don't want to end up with cream on the ceiling!).

Shake the jar up and down, so the cream sloshes around very vigorously inside.

Keep shaking.

Keep shaking.

No, really, keep shaking! After about 10 minutes of shaking (depending on how hard you shake), your cream should have turned into whipped cream. Keep going.

After about 15 minutes, the butter will start to separate from the buttermilk. Shake the jar until you have lots of little globules of firm butter floating in some very liquid buttermilk.

Pour the butter and buttermilk through a fine-mesh strainer. If you don't have a strainer, you can pour it into a bowl and fish the butter out with your hands. Press the little globules together to form one solid mass of butter. You'll probably need to squeeze it and knead it a few times to get all the buttermilk out.

That's it! Now you have fresh butter and fresh buttermilk. You can eat/drink them right away or store both in the fridge for future use. The butter will last up to 2 weeks, but the buttermilk goes bad faster and should be used or consumed within a few days.

Milk Bread

Makes Two 8½ by 4½-inch loaves

Difficulty level Intermediate

Time from start of mixing to baked bread 5 hours

Baking vessel Two 8½ by 4½-inch loaf pans

Mixer Needed

Ingredients

Scald

½ cup (118 grams) cold water

½ cup (118 grams) whole milk

⅓ cup (46 grams) all-purpose flour

This recipe makes a beautiful soft, fluffy loaf and uses an unusual technique to do so. Some of the flour in this bread is cooked with milk and water in order to create a scalded paste. This "scald" makes the bread extra soft and helps it last longer than a normal yeasted bread. This is a great go-to bread to make on the weekend for lunch box sandwiches and picnics.

Fun fact: The name for the cooked flour and water scald in Asia is *tangzhong*. This technique is the hallmark of Japanese milk bread but has also long been used in central European baking traditions.

To make the scald

In a small bowl, whisk together the cold water, whole milk, and flour until the mixture is smooth and there are no lumps.

Pour the mixture into a small saucepan and place it on a burner turned on to the low setting (get an adult assistant to help you with the stove if needed). Cook the mixture for 3 to 5 minutes, until it becomes thick. Stir it with a spatula or a wooden spoon continuously while it is cooking so that the mixture doesn't clump up. If it does clump a little, don't worry—just keep stirring.

Once the mixture has become thick and stiff, like pudding, remove the saucepan from the heat and set it aside to cool. Stir it occasionally while you are preparing the rest of the dough so that it cools evenly and does not form a dry skin on top.

Continued ⌇

Dough

1¼ cups (305 grams) whole milk, room temperature (about 75°F)

2 large eggs (120 grams total), room temperature

2 teaspoons (8 grams) instant dry yeast

⅓ cup (66 grams) granulated sugar

1 tablespoon (9 grams) kosher salt

4½ cups (630 grams) all-purpose flour

185 grams (¾ cup) scald (from above)

½ cup/1 stick (113 grams) unsalted butter, cut into tablespoons, room temperature

2 tablespoons unsalted butter, room temperature (or neutral oil), for greasing the pans

2 tablespoons whole milk, for brushing the top of the loaves before baking

To make the dough

Get a stand mixer fitted with a dough hook ready. Remove the bowl of the stand mixer and place the milk in the bowl. Crack the large eggs into the milk. Sprinkle the instant yeast over the milk and egg and whisk those three ingredients together. Add the sugar and salt into the milk, eggs, and yeast and whisk. (Check and stir the scald if you haven't yet!)

Next, add the flour to the mixer bowl. Place the bowl on the mixer with the dough hook and mix for 3 to 5 minutes, until the dough comes together. (Don't forget to stir your scald as it cools!) After the dough has come together, turn the mixer off for 5 minutes and let the flour hydrate and the gluten relax. (Stir that scald one more time.)

After 5 minutes, turn the mixer back on medium and mix for 5 more minutes, until the dough is a cohesive ball.

Add the scald. Turn the mixer off and add half of the scald. Turn the mixer back on low and mix for 2 to 3 minutes, until the scald is all incorporated. Turn the mixer off again and add the remaining scald. Turn the mixer back on low and mix for 1 minute, then on medium for 2 to 3 minutes, until all of the scald is incorporated into the dough.

Next, add the butter. You want to add it slowly, 1 tablespoon at a time. With the mixer off, add a tablespoon. Turn the mixer on medium again and mix for 1 minute, until the butter is mixed in. Then turn the mixer off, add another tablespoon, and turn it on medium again, mixing until the butter is thoroughly mixed in. Repeat these steps until all the butter is added.

After all the butter is added, mix on medium speed for 1 to 3 more minutes. The dough should be smooth, elastic, shiny, and a little sticky.

Next, you'll let the dough rise. Get a clean large mixing bowl and transfer the dough from the mixer bowl (which probably had gathered some crusties around the sides) to the clean bowl. Make sure the bowl is big enough for the dough to double in size.

Shaping

1. Scoop the dough out of the bowl and divide it

2. Pat out dough

3. Roll up dough

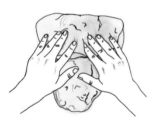

4. Pinch the seam shut

Let the dough rest at room temperature for 45 minutes.

After 45 minutes, fold the dough. This will even out the temperature, re-distribute areas of more activity, and strengthen the gluten. To do so, loosen it from the edges of the bowl. Lift the side of the dough up, stretch it over the top, and press it back down into the bowl. Do this a few times until you have lifted, stretched, and folded all the dough.

Let it rise again for 30 minutes to an hour, until it has again doubled in size. While it's finishing rising in the bowl, get two 8½ by 4½-inch bread pans ready by lightly greasing the sides. Use your fingers to smear 1 tablespoon butter evenly all over the inside of each pan (wash your hands well with warm water after you're done.) Alternatively, brush with neutral oil.

Once it has doubled in size, divide the dough. To divide the dough, scoop it out of the bowl (a bowl scraper is handy for this, but you can also use a spatula or just your fingers). Divide the dough equally in half using your bench knife to gently cut it. If you are using a scale, each half should weigh about 700 grams.

To shape the loaves, pat each portion of the dough gently into a rectangle, roughly 12 by 6 inches. The shorter sides of the rectangle should be at the top and bottom, and the longer sides should be on the right and left sides. Shape one loaf at a time: Using your fingertips, roll the top edge toward you, almost as if you're rolling up a carpet. Press the rolled part gently into the flat part as you continue to roll it toward you. Once it's all rolled up, press the seam together where the bottom edge meets the rolled-up part of the loaf. Place the shaped loaf into the pan with the seam on the bottom. Repeat with the second loaf.

Preheat the oven to 400°F and place a rack in the middle position (get an adult assistant to help if needed).

Continued ～

This bread is good for sandwiches, toast, French toast, and bread crumbs.

Cover the loaves loosely with clean linen and place in a warm, draft-free spot to rise for 30 minutes to 1 hour, until they have risen taller than the pans. If you poke a loaf gently with your fingertip, it should feel full of air and spring back slowly. Once they have risen, you're ready to bake.

Using a clean pastry brush, brush the top of the loaves with the milk so that they are evenly coated.

Next, score the loaves (for more about scoring, see page 159). Use some sharp kitchen scissors (get an adult assistant to help if needed) to snip the top six to eight times. Alternatively, use a sharp knife to make small slits or slashes in the top of the loaf.

Once the loaves have been brushed with milk and scored, you are ready to put them in the oven. Place the pans gently on the rack in the middle of the oven (get an adult assistant to help if needed). Close the oven door and set a timer for 20 minutes.

After 20 minutes, take a peek at your loaves. If it looks like one part of the loaf is darker, use oven mitts to turn the pans half a turn so that they will finish baking evenly (get an adult assistant to help if needed).

Bake for 10 to 15 more minutes. The loaves are finished when they are medium brown all over the top. If they look speckled or blonde, give them a few more minutes.

When they're done baking, use oven mitts to remove the pan from the oven (get an adult assistant to help if needed). Set the pans on a heatproof surface (such as a stovetop) to cool for 10 minutes.

After 10 minutes, gently remove the loaves from the pans (get an adult assistant to help if needed). Set the loaves on a cooling rack and let cool for at least 1 hour.

This bread stays soft for days (thanks to that scald). You can keep it in a bread box or bag on the countertop for up to 4 days. If it starts to feel stale, you can cut slices and toast them. To store it for longer, slice it and keep it in a sealed container in the freezer. To serve, take as many slices as you'd like from the freezer and toast them.

This bread is good for toast, French toast, sandwiches, and bread crumbs.

Brioche

with variations for Morning Bun Monkey Bread and Cocoa Swirl Bread

Makes Two 8½ x 4½-inch loaves or 18 brioche à tête

Difficulty level Intermediate

Time from start of mixing to baked bread 6 hours (plus 3 hours ahead to prepare the sponge)

Baking vessel Two 8½ x 4½-inch bread pans

Mixer Needed

Brioche is a classic French bread, known for being very rich. It is often used for desserts or as an element in sweet or savory recipes. Cut into small pieces and rolled into balls, it makes great sandwich buns. Brioche à tête is a classic French shape, baked in little fluted tins with a round ball of dough on top (*à tête* means "with a head"). I've included two fun variations here. One is Morning Bun Monkey Bread, in which you roll small balls of brioche in morning bun sugar and bake it in a pan for a pull-apart treats. The other is for a Cocoa Swirl Loaf.

Ingredients

Sponge (make 3 hours ahead)

1⅔ cups (400 grams) warm whole milk (about 85°F)

½ teaspoon (2 grams) instant dry yeast

3 cups (420 grams) all-purpose flour

To make the sponge

Measure the warm milk into a medium bowl (make sure there is plenty of room for it to grow). Sprinkle the yeast on top of it, then stir to dissolve the yeast. Add the flour, stirring until well combined. Cover and let rest on the countertop in a warm, draft-free spot for 3 hours. It's ready to use when it has doubled in size and is very bubbly.

Continued ∽

63

Brioche
Continued ~

Dough

¾ cup (180 grams) warm whole milk (about 85°F)

½ teaspoon (2 grams) instant dry yeast

9 cups (431 grams) sponge

3 medium eggs (180 grams total), room temperature

1 egg yolk (22 grams), room temperature

3 cups (420 grams) all-purpose flour

2½ tablespoons (28 grams) granulated sugar

1 tablespoon (9 grams) kosher salt

1 cup or 2 sticks (227 grams) unsalted butter, cut into tablespoons, softened, plus 2 tablespoons for greasing the pans (or use neutral oil for greasing)

2 tablespoons whole milk, for brushing the top of the loaf

NOTE You want the butter to be soft enough to mix easily into the dough, but if it's too soft it won't incorporate properly. Try to warm the butter just enough that you can easily dent it with a finger, but not so warm that it's soft and squishy.

To make the dough

Place the warm milk, yeast, sponge, eggs, yolk, flour, sugar, and salt in the bowl of a stand mixer fitted with the dough hook attachment. Mix on low speed until everything is well combined and a dough starts to form, about 3 minutes. Let the dough rest for 3 minutes.

After 3 minutes, mix on medium speed for about 5 minutes, until the dough is strong and supple.

With the mixer on medium, add the butter, 1 tablespoon at a time. Wait until each addition of butter is completely incorporated and the dough has come back together before adding the next. Add the butter slowly this way, mixing the whole time, until all the butter is incorporated. Mix for 3 to 5 more minutes after all the butter is incorporated, until the dough is smooth, supple, and shiny.

Remove the dough from the mixing bowl and place it in a clean bowl, with room to double in size. Place it in a warm, draft-free spot and allow to rest for 30 minutes.

After 30 minutes, fold the dough. This will even out the temperature, re-distribute areas of more activity, and strengthen the gluten. To do so, loosen it from the edges of the bowl. Lift the side of the dough up, stretch it over the top, and press it back down into the bowl. Do this a few times until you have lifted, stretched, and folded all the dough. Cover the dough bowl again and let rest for 30 more minutes to an hour.

After this last rest, it should have risen noticeably in the bowl. You should be able to see bubbles in the dough. If you can see the rising and the bubbles, it's time to divide the dough. If not, let it rest for 15 more minutes. Check the dough every 10 to 15 minutes and divide it when you see a dramatic increase in size and lots of bubbles.

While it's finishing rising in the bowl, get two 8½ by 4½-inch rectangular bread pans ready by lightly buttering the sides. Use your fingers or a pastry brush to spread the soft butter evenly all over the inside of the pans. Alternatively, brush with neutral oil.

Shaping

1. Scoop the dough out of the bowl and divide it

2. Pat out dough

3. Roll up dough

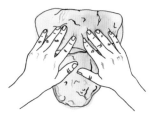

4. Pinch the seam shut

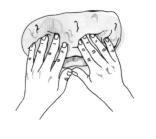

To divide the dough, scoop it out of the bowl (a bowl scraper is handy for this, but you can also use a spatula or just your fingers). Divide the dough equally in half using your bench knife to gently cut it. If you are using a scale, each half should weigh about 700 grams.

To shape the loaves, pat each portion of the dough gently into a rectangle, roughly 12 by 6 inches. The shorter sides of the rectangle should be at the top and bottom, and the longer sides should be on the right and left sides. Shape one loaf at a time. Using your fingertips, roll the top edge toward you, almost as if you're rolling up a carpet. Press the rolled part gently into the flat part as you continue to roll it toward you. Once it's all rolled up, press the seam together where the bottom edge meets the rolled-up part of the loaf. Place the shaped loaf into the pan with the seam on the bottom. Repeat with the second loaf.

Preheat the oven to 400°F and place a rack in the middle position of the oven (get an adult assistant to help if needed).

Cover the loaves loosely with a clean linen and place in a warm, draft-free spot to let rise for 30 minutes to 1 hour, until they have risen taller than the loaf pans. If you poke a loaf gently with your fingertip, it should feel full of air and spring back slowly. Once they have risen in the pans, you're ready to bake.

Using a clean pastry brush, brush the top of the loaves with milk so that they are evenly coated.

Next, score the loaves (for more about scoring, see page 159). Use some sharp kitchen scissors to snip the top six to eight times (get an adult assistant to help if needed). Alternatively, use a sharp knife to make small slits or slashes in the top of the loaf.

Once the loaves have been brushed with milk and scored, you are ready to put them in the oven. Place the pans gently on the rack in the middle of the oven (get an adult assistant to help if needed). Close the oven door and set a timer for 20 minutes.

Continued 〜

After 20 minutes, take a peek at your loaves. If it looks like one part of the loaf is darker, use oven mitts to turn the pans half a turn so that they will finish baking evenly (get an adult assistant if needed).

Bake for 10 to 15 more minutes. The loaves are finished baking when they are an even medium brown all over the top. If they look speckled or blonde, give them a few more minutes.

When they are done baking, use oven mitts to remove the pans from the oven (get an adult assistant to help if needed.) Set the pans on a heatproof surface (such as a stovetop) to cool for 10 minutes.

After 10 minutes, gently remove the loaves from the pans (get an adult assistant to help if needed). Set the loaves on a cooling rack and let cool for at least 1 hour.

This bread is best if eaten fresh within a day. After the first day, you can cut slices and toast them (this bread makes dreamy toast). To store it for longer, slice it and keep it in a sealed container in the freezer. To serve, take as many slices as you'd like from the freezer and toast them.

Other brioche variations
Brioche dough is the basis for so many things . . .

brioche à tête

braided brioche

brioche buns

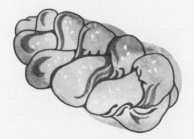

Morning Bun Monkey Bread

Makes One 8-inch round pan of monkey bread

Ingredients

1 recipe brioche dough (page 63)

Morning bun sugar

1 cup packed light brown sugar

Zest of 1 orange, grated on a fine Microplane

1 tablespoon cinnamon

2 tablespoons butter, room temperature, for greasing the pan

2 tablespoons superfine or granulated sugar for sprinkling the pan

Confectioners' or superfine sugar, for dusting

One of my favorite things that the bakers at Tartine make is the morning buns. The gooey-sweet combination of sugar, orange zest, and cinnamon is irresistible. They are made with croissant dough, which is an advanced dough that involves delicate temperature balances and elaborate rolling and folding. This monkey bread is a great way to get the same flavors with a bit less fuss over the dough.

Superfine sugar is a finer granulated sugar. It melts a little more easily than granulated sugar does in the oven and makes the edges of this monkey bread extra gooey. When you sprinkle a little on after, it doesn't melt as easily as confectioners' sugar but gives you a slightly sparkly finish. It's a nice treat if you can find it, but I've given options for substitutions in case you can't.

Prepare one 8-inch round cake pan or other ovenproof pan or skillet. Butter the sides generously with softened butter and sprinkle with superfine or granulated sugar.

To make the morning bun sugar

In a large mixing bowl, mix together the sugar, orange zest, and cinnamon until well combined and set aside.

To prepare the monkey bread

Prepare the brioche up until the point that you are ready to shape it. Instead of shaping the dough into a loaf shape, roll or pat it out to a 1-inch thickness on your work surface. Let the dough rest for 5 minutes, then cut it into 1-inch pieces. The dough should not be sticky—try to pat it out without using any flour (or only a bare minimum) so that the sugar sticks.

Toss the pieces of brioche dough in the morning bun sugar so that they are evenly coated. Place them in the buttered and sugared pan, stacking and filling it to the top. Place in a warm, draft-free spot, cover, and proof for 30 minutes, until the monkey bread has risen well above the top of the pan.

During this final proofing, preheat the oven to 400°F and place a rack in the middle position (get an adult assistant to help if needed).

When the monkey bread has risen and is ready to bake, use oven mitts to place it carefully in the preheated oven (ask an adult assistant to help if needed). Set a timer for 20 minutes.

After 20 minutes, check to see if it is baking evenly. If one side is browning faster, use your oven mitts to rotate the pan (ask an adult assistant for help if needed).

Bake for another 5 minutes or so, until it is well browned on top.

Once it is done baking, use your oven mitts to remove it from the oven (get an adult assistant to help if needed). Set the pan on a heatproof surface (such as a stovetop) and let cool for about 10 minutes. Sprinkle superfine or confectioners' sugar over the top.

This is best served warm and can be kept in a sealed container for up to 2 days. Reheat it in a 400°F oven for about 10 minutes before serving.

Cocoa Swirl Bread

Makes Two 8½ x 4½-inch loaves

Ingredients

1 recipe brioche dough (page 63)

Filling

½ cup heavy cream

½ cup packed light brown sugar

1 cup dark chocolate pieces (chips, feves, or finely chopped baking bar)

1 tablespoon cinnamon

This became a favorite of my kids during the testing phase of this book, and now it's a staple weekend brunch treat in our house. The combination of the spiced dark chocolate and the rich, buttery brioche makes a truly decadent toast.

Prepare the brioche dough until the step before you are ready to shape it.

To make the filling

While the dough is undergoing its final rise, prepare the filling. To do so, warm the cream in a medium saucepan. Add the brown sugar and stir to dissolve. Add the chocolate and let it melt. Stir in the cinnamon. Don't worry if all the sugar doesn't melt all the way. Set aside and allow the mixture to come to room temperature.

To make the bread

Once the dough is divided into two portions, pat the first one out to a rectangle 1 inch thick and about 6 inches wide and 12 inches long. Spread half the chocolate filling evenly over the dough, leaving a 1-inch gap on the side closest to you. Starting at the top, roll the dough toward you gently (try not to stretch it as you roll, as this can cause the filling to drop away from the bread when it's baking.) Roll it up all the way. Seal the bottom (where you left the gap with no filling) and place the loaf, seam side down, in a buttered loaf pan. Repeat with the remaining dough and filling.

Bake the same way as for brioche.

Challah

Makes One large, braided challah

Difficulty level
Intermediate (shaping)

Time from start of mixing to baked bread 5 hours

Baking vessel Sheet pan

Mixer Needed

Ingredients

1 cup (236 grams) warm water (about 85°F)

1 teaspoon (4 grams) instant dry yeast

¼ cup (54 grams) sunflower seed oil

2 medium eggs (130 grams total), room temperature, + 1 egg for the egg wash

¼ cup (50 grams) granulated sugar

1 tablespoon (9 grams) kosher salt, plus a pinch for the egg wash

3⅔ cups (513 grams) all-purpose flour

Poppy seeds or sesame seeds, for sprinkling (optional)

Challah is a Jewish bread, often served for Sabbath meals or ceremonial occasions. It is traditionally shaped so that the twelve strands represent the twelve tribes of Israel. Challah that is used for rituals has a small portion set aside as an offering. There are variations of braided breads all over North Africa and Eastern Europe, but this is one that will be familiar to any communities around the Jewish diaspora.

I was lucky enough as a kid to have a very good friend who was Jewish. Her mom was an excellent cook, and eating matzo soup, latkes, and challah at her table are some of my favorite childhood memories. I also worked at Noah's Bagels in high school and snacked on the challah at work more often than the bagels. This bread, while not part of my historical familial heritage, will always hold special nostalgia for me. I offer this recipe humbly, with reverence for ancient tradition.

In the bowl of a stand mixer, measure the warm water and yeast. You can remove the bowl from the mixer and do this part by hand. Whisk to dissolve the yeast. Add the oil and whisk it in. Add the 2 eggs, one at a time, whisking each one in before adding the next. Add the sugar and salt and whisk to dissolve.

Measure the flour into the bowl and place the bowl back on the mixer, fitted with the dough hook attachment.

Mix on low speed for 3 minutes. Check to make sure all the ingredients are combined well by scraping the bottom of the bowl with a spatula. Let rest for 3 minutes.

After 3 minutes, mix on medium for 5 to 7 minutes, until the dough is smooth, strong, and supple.

Continued ∿

This bread is wonderful served warm and fresh. It makes a gorgeous centerpiece for a friends and/or family meal.

Remove the bowl from the mixer and scrape the sides clean with your plastic dough scraper. Cover the bowl with a clean linen and let rest for 1 hour in a warm spot.

After 1 hour, fold the dough. This will even out the temperature, re-distribute areas of more activity, and strengthen the gluten. To do so, loosen it from the edges of the bowl. Lift the side of the dough up, stretch it over the top, and press it back down into the bowl. Do this a few times until you have lifted, stretched, and folded all the dough. Let rest for 30 minutes.

After 30 minutes, the dough should have risen noticeably in the bowl. You should be able to see bubbles in the dough and at the edges or top of the dough. If you can see the rising and the bubbles, it's time to divide the dough. If not, let it rest for 15 more minutes. Check the dough every 10 to 15 minutes and divide it when you see an increase in size and bubbles. When it's ready, use a dough scraper to scrape the dough out of the bowl and onto a very lightly floured work surface.

One of the tricks to getting the challah braid to look nice is to shape even "ropes" of dough to braid. If you have a scale, use it to weigh out six portions of dough at about 165 grams each. If not, try to divide the dough into six portions as evenly as you possibly can. Roll each piece of dough out into a rope approximately 10 inches long. Let rest for 10 minutes (it's easier to braid if the gluten relaxes a little.)

After 10 minutes, you can do either two three-stranded braids (just like for hair) or a six-stranded braid.

To do a six-stranded braid, pinch all six of the ropes together at the top. Cross the two outer ropes over each other at the top to start the braid.

1 Bring the outer left-hand rope into the center and lay it down.

2 Bring the second rope from the right all the way to the outer left and lay it down.

To do a three-stranded braid, pinch three of the ropes of dough together at the top. Braid the dough by taking the right-hand rope and laying it over the middle rope, then take the left rope and lay it over the middle rope (so the right becomes the middle, then the left becomes the middle.) Continue until the whole rope is braided. Repeat with the remaining three ropes. Nestle the two braids next to each other on a sheet pan and pinch the ends of the two braids together.

Six-Stranded Braid

1

2

3

4

3 Bring the outer right-hand rope into the center and lay it down.

4 Bring the second rope from the left all the way over to the outer right and lay it down.

Repeat steps 1–4 until the whole rope is braided. Pinch the tops and the bottoms together and roll them back and forth a little if needed to seal the braid. Place the braided challah on a sheet pan.

Allow the loaf to rise for 1 hour in a warm, draft-free spot. Cover lightly with a clean, dry linen or spritz with a spray bottle of clean, warm water occasionally to keep the dough from forming a dry skin.

Once the challah is proofed, apply an egg wash. To do so, crack the remaining egg into a small bowl. Mix it very well until the yolk and the white are completely combined. Add a tiny pinch of salt and mix that in. Use a pastry brush to brush the egg wash evenly over the top of the challah. If you want, you can sprinkle poppy seeds or sesame seeds (or anything else you like) over the egg wash at this time.

Preheat the oven to 375°F and place the rack in the middle position (ask an adult assistant for help if needed).

After the loaf has risen and been brushed with egg wash, use oven mitts to place it carefully in the oven (ask an adult assistant for help if needed). Set a timer for 20 minutes.

After 20 minutes, check to see if the challah needs to be rotated to finish baking evenly. If one side is browning faster, wear your oven mitts and rotate the sheet pan (ask an adult assistant for help if needed). Bake for 10 to 20 more minutes, until golden brown all over.

Once the challah is done baking and a tester comes out clean, use oven mitts to remove the pan from the oven (ask an adult assistant for help if needed) and place the tray on a heatproof surface (such as the stovetop). Let it cool for about 5 minutes on the pan, then use a spatula (or two) to move it to a cooling rack. Let cool until just warm to the touch.

This bread is good for sandwiches; serving with extra-virgin olive oil for dipping as a snack, appetizer, or side; or cut in half lengthwise, topped with sauce and cheese, and placed under the broiler for a great French bread–style "pizza."

Focaccia

Makes One 8-inch focaccia

Difficulty level
Intermediate

**Time from start of mixing
to baked bread** 5 hours
for dough (plus 3 hours
ahead to prepare the
sponge)

Baking vessel An 8-inch
cast-iron skillet (or an
18 by 13 inch sheet pan)

Mixer Needed

Ingredients

Sponge
(make 3 hours ahead)

½ cup (118 grams) cool
water (about 70°F)

½ teaspoon (2 grams)
instant dry yeast

¾ cup (105 grams)
bread flour

Focaccia is an Italian flatbread. It usually has herbs,
spices, tomatoes, and/or other decoratively cut vegetables
added to the top. The toppings can be as simple as a
sprinkle of sea salt or as complex as an array of spring
vegetables. Sturdy herbs like rosemary are a classic
choice. Focaccia is like a crispy golden canvas that you
can paint on with food to make beautiful edible art

This focaccia uses the sponge method (see page 37). Using
a sponge improves three things: flavor, texture, and the
amount of time your bread lasts before going stale. This is
a great one to try with an overnight sponge—just let it sit
out for an hour, put in the fridge overnight, then let it come
to room temperature for about an hour before using.

To make the sponge

In a medium mixing bowl, measure the cool water.
Sprinkle the yeast on top of the water. Stir with a spoon
to dissolve the yeast. Add the flour to the bowl. Stir with a
wooden spoon or your hand until the flour and water are
combined well and there are no lumps. Cover the mixing
bowl with a clean linen and let rest in a warm, draft-free
spot for 3 hours. It's ready to use when it has doubled in
size and is very bubbly.

Continued ～

Focaccia

1½ cups (354 grams) warm water (about 85°F)

½ teaspoon (2 grams) instant dry yeast

2 teaspoons (9 grams) extra-virgin olive oil, plus 1 tablespoon each for the bowl and skillet

1 tablespoon + 1 teaspoon (12 grams) kosher salt

2½ cups (213 grams) sponge

3 cups (420 grams) bread flour

Toppings

½ cup fresh basil

⅓ cup fresh oregano

1 pint fresh cherry tomatoes

2 tablespoons extra-virgin olive oil

Sprinkle of flaky sea salt

To make the focaccia

In the bowl of a stand mixer fitted with the dough hook, measure the warm water. Sprinkle the yeast over the water and mix on low for 1 minute to dissolve the yeast. Add the 2 teaspoons olive oil and kosher salt and mix to combine.

Add the sponge and the flour. Mix on low for 3 minutes until all ingredients are combined well. Let it rest for 3 minutes.

After 3 minutes, mix it on medium speed for 3 more minutes. Let it rest for 3 minutes.

After 3 minutes, mix it again for 3 to 5 minutes, until the dough is very smooth and stretchy.

Get a clean medium bowl and pour 1 tablespoon of olive oil into it. Use your fingers to spread the olive oil so that it coats the bowl. Scoop the dough out of the mixing bowl and into the olive oil–coated bowl. Cover the bowl with the dough with a clean linen and let the dough rest for 30 minutes.

After 30 minutes, fold the dough. This will even out the temperature, re-distribute areas of more activity, and strengthen the gluten. To do so, loosen it from the edges of the bowl. Lift the side of the dough up, stretch it over the top, and press it back down into the bowl. Do this a few times until you have lifted, stretched, and folded all the dough.

Cover the dough bowl again and let rest for 30 more minutes.

After 30 minutes, fold the dough again. Cover and let rest for 30 more minutes to 1 hour.

While the dough is resting, prepare your toppings. Chop the basil finely with a sharp knife and pick the oregano leaves off the stems. Cut the tomatoes in half and set aside.

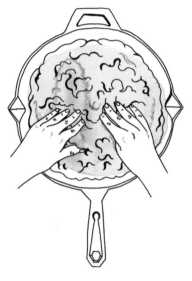

After 30 minutes to 1 hour, the dough should be visibly bigger than it was when you folded it. When you pull it away from the sides, you should be able to see some air bubbles—it might look almost like a honeycomb. This means it's ready to move on to the next step.

Preheat the oven to 450°F and place a rack in the middle position (get an adult assistant to help if needed).

Prepare your baking skillet. Pour 1 tablespoon olive oil into an 8-inch ovenproof skillet and swirl it around (or use your fingers to spread it) so that it covers the bottom of the skillet.

Use wet fingers and a plastic bowl scraper to loosen the dough from the bowl. Scoop the dough from the bowl straight into the skillet. Pour 2 tablespoons of olive oil over the top of the dough. Use your fingers to spread the dough into the skillet. Press your fingertips deeply into the dough over the whole thing to get that distinctive bubbly focaccia top.

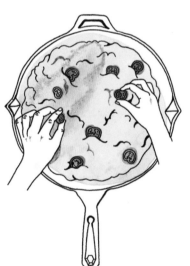

Place the tomatoes on top, pressing them into the dough a little. They should be sitting firmly on top of the dough but not poked all the way down into it. You can place them randomly or make a pattern or design—this part's up to you!

Let the topped dough rest for 45 minutes to 1½ hours. You don't need to cover it, as the coating of olive oil over the top will keep it from drying out, but do keep it someplace warm.

After 45 minutes to 1½ hours, the dough should be much taller and bubblier. This means it's ready to bake. If it hasn't grown dramatically, let it continue to rise until it has. Right before you're ready to bake it, sprinkle some flaky sea salt over the top.

Using oven mitts, carefully place the skillet of dough in the oven (get an adult assistant to help if needed). Set a timer for 20 minutes.

Continued 〜

After 20 minutes, take a peek at the focaccia. If it's darker brown on one side than the other, use oven mitts to rotate the skillet so that it bakes evenly (get an adult assistant to help if needed.)

Bake for 10 more minutes. The focaccia should be a golden brown color. If it is still light golden or just speckled with brown, let it bake for 5 more minutes, or until it is golden brown.

Once the focaccia is done baking, use oven mitts to remove the skillet carefully from the oven. Place the skillet on a heatproof surface (such as the stovetop) to cool for 5 minutes. (Get an adult assistant to help if needed.)

After 5 minutes, use your oven mitts to carefully loosen the focaccia from the skillet. A butter knife or metal spatula can be helpful for this. Once it's loose, use the knife or spatula as a lever to pop the bread out of the skillet. If it's really stuck and doesn't want to come out or if it's still just too hot, let it rest for 5 more minutes and try again. Sprinkle the basil and oregano over the warm focaccia. Once it's out, set it on a cooling rack until cool enough to eat.

This bread can be kept in a paper bag or a bread box on the counter for up to 3 days. It should be reheated under a broiler before serving if it's more than 24 hours old.

This bread is good for crusty sandwiches, "French bread" pizza, dipping in extra-virgin olive oil or hummus, and drizzling with honey

Ciabatta

Ciabatta is another Italian bread. At first glance, it looks similar to focaccia, but its purpose is a little different. Ciabatta is treated more like a free-form loaf, used for sandwiches or for scooping and sopping, as opposed to a focaccia, which is baked with the additions on top and often eaten solo—more like a fluffy pizza. The word *ciabatta* in Italian translates to "slipper" in English—the loaf almost looks like a squishy, comfy slipper when it comes out of the oven.

Ciabatta dough is intentionally very wet (high hydration, in bread bakers' terms). This gives it large, craggy, open holes in the crumb and a thin, shattering crust. We tend to think of ciabatta as an iconic, classic Italian bread, but the word *ciabatta* wasn't used as a name for bread until the 1980s! This style of high-hydration, craggy bread is much older, though.

Makes Two 700-gram flat loaves

Difficulty level Intermediate (wet dough)

Time from start of mixing to baked bread 6 hours (plus 3 hours ahead to prepare the sponge)

Mixer Needed

Baking vessel Baking steel or stone

Ingredients

Sponge (make 3 hours ahead)

1½ cups (354 grams) cool water (about 70°F)

½ teaspoon (2 grams) instant dry yeast

2½ cups (350 grams) bread flour

To make the sponge

In a medium mixing bowl, measure the cool water. Sprinkle the yeast on top of the water. Stir with a spoon to dissolve the yeast in the water. Add the flour to the bowl. Stir with a wooden spoon or your hand until the flour and water are combined well and there are no lumps. Cover the mixing bowl with a clean linen and let rest on the countertop for three hours. It's ready to use when it has doubled in size and is very bubbly.

Continued ∿

Dough

2½ cups (590 grams) warm
water (about 85°F)

2 teaspoons (8 grams)
instant dry yeast

8 cups (722 grams) sponge

1 tablespoon + 1 teaspoon
(12 grams) kosher salt

¼ cup (54 grams) extra-
virgin olive oil, plus
1 teaspoon for the bowl

5¼ cups (735 grams)
bread flour

To make the dough

**In the bowl of a stand mixer fitted with the dough
hook, measure the warm water.** Sprinkle the yeast over
the water and mix on low for 1 minute to dissolve the
yeast. Add the salt, sponge, and ¼ cup olive oil and mix
to combine.

Add the flour. Mix on low speed for about 3 minutes, until
everything is combined. Let rest for 3 minutes.

**After 3 minutes, mix it on medium speed for 3 more
minutes.** Let it rest for 3 minutes.

After 3 minutes, mix it again for 3 to 5 minutes, until the
dough is very smooth and stretchy

**In a clean medium bowl, pour the remaining 1 teaspoon
olive oil.** Use your fingers to spread the olive oil so that it
coats the bowl. Scoop the dough out of the mixing bowl
and into the olive oil–coated bowl. Cover with a clean
linen and let the dough rest in a warm, draft-free spot for
30 minutes.

After 30 minutes, fold the dough. This will even out the
temperature, re-distribute areas of more activity, and
strengthen the gluten. To do so, loosen it from the edges
of the bowl. Lift the side of the dough up, stretch it over
the top, and press it back down into the bowl. Do this a
few times until you have lifted, stretched, and folded all
the dough.

**Cover the dough bowl again and let rest for 30 more
minutes.**

After 30 minutes, fold the dough again. Cover and let rest
for 30 more minutes to 1 hour.

**After 30 minutes to 1 hour, the dough should have doubled
in size.** When you pull it away from the sides, you should
be able to see some air bubbles—it might look almost like
a honeycomb. This means it's ready to move on to the
next step.

**Place the baking steel or stone on the middle rack in the
oven and preheat it to 475°F** (get an adult assistant to help
if needed).

Prepare a clean piece of linen by spreading it flat on your work surface and flouring it *very* liberally. Use wet fingers and a plastic bowl scraper to loosen the dough from the bowl. Divide the dough in half and shape each half into a rectangle. This doesn't have to be perfect at all—it's supposed to be kind of free-form. Place each rectangle on the well-floured linen and let rest for 45 minutes to 1 hour, until it has increased noticeably in size.

After 45 minutes to 1 hour, gently transfer one loaf to a baguette peel (see Peels on page 34). Score the top of the loaf by snipping it a few times with a pair of scissors or by slicing shallowly with a sharp knife (get an adult assistant to help if needed).

Using oven mitts, carefully open the oven and gently slide the loaf off the baguette peel and onto the hot baking steel or stone (get an adult assistant to help if needed). Depending on how big your baking steel is, you may be able to bake both ciabattas at once. If not, bake them one at a time. Set a timer for 15 minutes.

After 15 minutes, take a peek at the ciabatta. If it's darker brown on one side than the other, use a spatula to rotate the loaves so that the ciabatta bakes evenly (get an adult assistant to help if needed).

Bake for 5 to 10 more minutes. The ciabatta should be a golden brown color. If it is still very light or just barely speckled with blonde, let it bake for 5 more minutes.

Once the loaves are done baking, use a spatula to remove the loaves carefully from the oven. Let rest on a cooling rack until just warm to the touch before eating.

This bread can be kept in a paper bag or a bread box on the counter for up to 3 days. It should be reheated under a broiler before serving if it's more than 24 hours old.

Pizza Dough

Makes Four 8-inch pies

Difficulty level Beginner dough, intermediate shaping and baking

Time from start of mixing to finished pizza 6 hours (plus 3 hours ahead to prepare the sponge)

Baking vessel Pizza steel or stone

Mixer Optional

Pizza is easily one of my favorite things to make. Maybe that's because it is one of my favorite things to eat, but I also enjoy the process of stretching, topping, and baking the pies almost as much as eating them. Making pizza is one of the most fun, versatile, and forgiving things you can do with flour and water.

There are many different kinds of pizzas: square, round, thick, thin, crispy, and chewy. I like mine with a lot of whole wheat in the dough, stretched thinner in the middle and fluffy on the edges.

One of the most important things to getting a pizza-baking session to run smoothly is setting up a pizza-making station (see more about mise en place on page 12). Once you start making your pizzas, you'll want to stretch and shape them, top them, and bake them as quickly as possible. If you let the dough sit too long, you run a greater risk of the pizza getting sticky or tearing.

I like to have all my ingredients ready during the final stage of resting the dough and set up my pizza-making station. I clean and trim or slice anything that needs it, like greens, onions, mushrooms, or tomatoes. Anything else I want to add, like tomato sauce, cheese, or meat, is all opened or out of the package and ready to go. I have a set of small bowls I like to use for this.

One of the other tricky parts of pizza making is getting the hang of scooting the pizza off the peel (see Peels on page 34) and onto the baking surface. If you've never done this before, try putting a folded dish towel onto the peel and practice scooting it off onto a target, like a place mat. Eventually, you'll get good enough that you can scoot the whole thing off quickly and in very few movements, leaving the pizza sitting perfectly round on the baking surface.

Continued ～

Ingredients

Sponge
(make 3 hours ahead)

1 cup (236 grams) warm
 water (about 85°F)

½ teaspoon (2 grams)
 instant dry yeast

½ cup (70 grams) whole
 wheat flour

1⅔ cups (233 grams)
 bread flour

Dough

1 cup + 2 tablespoons
 (266 grams) warm water
 (about 85°F)

½ teaspoon (2 grams)
 instant dry yeast

2 teaspoons (9 grams)
 extra-virgin olive oil, plus
 1 teaspoon for the bowl

1 tablespoon (9 grams)
 kosher salt

6⅓ cups (300 grams)
 sponge

2 cups + 2 tablespoons
 (308 grams) bread flour

¾ cup (105 grams) whole
 wheat flour

All-purpose flour, for
 coating the dough balls

Semolina flour, for dusting
 the peel

To make the sponge

Pour the warm water into a medium mixing bowl—make sure there is plenty of room in it for the sponge to grow. Sprinkle the yeast on top. Stir with a spoon to dissolve the yeast in the water. Add both flours to the bowl. Stir with a wooden spoon or your hand until the flour and water are combined well and there are no lumps. Cover the mixing bowl with a clean dish towel and let rest on the countertop in a warm, draft-free spot for 3 hours. It's ready to use when it has doubled in size and is very bubbly.

To make the dough

In a large mixing bowl (or the bowl of a stand mixer, removed from the mixer) measure the warm water, yeast, 2 teaspoons olive oil, salt, and sponge. Stir to combine.

Add the bread flour and the whole wheat flour. Use your hand (or the mixer fitted with the dough hook) to mix the ingredients together until they form a dough. Let rest for 3 minutes.

After 3 minutes, mix the dough for 3 minutes. Stir and fold the dough together, using your hand like a hook to stretch and fold the dough. Alternatively, place the dough in the bowl of a stand mixer with the dough hook attached and mix on medium speed for 3 minutes. Let rest for 3 minutes.

After 3 minutes, mix it again for 3 to 5 minutes, still using your hand like a hook to stretch and fold the dough. If the dough is in a mixer bowl, mix on medium speed again for 3 to 5 minutes.

Get a clean medium bowl and pour the remaining 1 teaspoon olive oil into it. Use your fingers to spread the olive oil so that it coats the bowl. Scoop the dough out of the mixing bowl and into the olive oil-coated bowl. Cover with a clean linen and let the dough rest for 30 minutes.

After 30 minutes, fold the dough. This will even out the temperature, re-distribute areas of more activity, and strengthen the gluten. To do so, loosen it from the edges of the bowl. Lift the side of the dough up, stretch it over the top, and press it back down into the bowl. Do this a few times until you have lifted, stretched, and folded all the dough.

Cover it again and let it rest for 30 minutes.

After 30 minutes, fold the dough one more time.

Cover it again and let it rest for 30 minutes to 1 hour. After this last rest, it should have risen noticeably in the bowl. You should be able to see bubbles at the edges or top of the dough. If you can see the rising and the bubbles, it's time to divide the dough. If not, let it rest for 15 more minutes. Check the dough every 10 to 15 minutes and divide it when you see a dramatic increase in size and lots of bubbles.

While the dough is resting, prepare your mise en place—any toppings you want for the pizza. As soon as the pizza has been stretched into its circular shape, you'll want to get the toppings on it and load it into the oven as quickly as possible so that it doesn't stick.

Once it has doubled in size, scoop the dough out of the bowl onto a clean work surface. To shape the dough balls, divide the dough into four equal pieces. Place one ball on a clean, unfloured work surface in front of you. Cup your hands around it and roll the dough in a circular motion, making it as round and as even as you can. Repeat this with all the dough pieces.

Let them rest for 30 minutes to 1 hour. You can also refrigerate them overnight or up to 72 hours at this point.

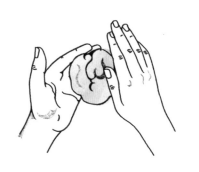

While the balls are resting (or whenever you're ready to make the pizza, if you've chilled the balls), preheat the oven to 500°F and place a baking steel or stone in middle position (get an adult assistant to help if needed). Pizza bakes best in a super-hot oven, but this also means you need to be extra careful. If you're uncomfortable with using this much heat, you can lower the temp to 450°F and extend the cooking time by a few minutes.

Continued ∿

When you're ready to make the pizzas, take one dough ball and flour the whole thing well. I like to dip it in a bowl of all-purpose flour. Place the dough ball on the worktable in front of you and pat it out into a flat disk with your fingers.

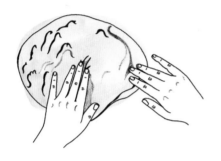

There are two ways to finish the pizza shape. One is to leave the disk on the worktable and stretch it wide and flat by pressing down on it with your fingertips. This is an easier way and the first way you should try. Be patient with it—remember that gluten relaxes over time, so if you aren't getting it as big as you want, just let it rest for a minute and come back to it. If you like, you can pick it up and pull on it to get it thin and round. Stretch it pretty wide and pretty thin—remember it will puff up in the oven. Flour any sticky spots as you go. Remember also that it doesn't have to be perfect. Oblong, heart-shaped, and triangular pizzas are also super delicious. Your tongue won't tell the difference.

The other way is to stretch it over the back of your hands and your fingers. This way will get you a thinner, larger pizza, but it's also trickier. To stretch it over the back of your hands, pick up that disk you pressed out with your fingertips and drape it over the back of your hands and your fingers. Slowly spread your fingers and your hands apart, gently stretching the dough. Rotate it a little (I usually go counterclockwise, but it doesn't matter) and stretch a little more. Keep going until it is as wide and thin as you want. Pay attention to what's happening to the dough—stretch it where it's thicker and skip over parts that are already thin. If it tears, just set it down on your work surface and press the sides of the tear together to repair it. Flour any sticky spots as you go. As above, remember it doesn't have to be perfect. Embrace whatever shape you end up with, and know that as you practice, you'll get better and better at achieving what you imagine.

Once you have your dough ball shaped and stretched into a flat pizza shape, sprinkle your peel with semolina flour and place the pizza dough on it. Move it around until you're happy with the shape.

To add your toppings

Start with the tomato sauce. Put a generous spoonful in the middle of the pizza dough and spread it thinly around with the back of the spoon. Leave ½ inch on the outside of the circle for the crust. Don't spoon too much pizza sauce on or the dough will become too wet and soggy when you're baking it. Strategically place a few tablespoon-size pieces of mozzarella around the pizza. Drizzle a little olive oil over the whole thing and sprinkle very lightly with sea salt.

You're ready to bake. Carefully open the oven, place the peel over the baking surface, and quickly shimmy the pizza off the peel and onto the baking surface in a swift forward motion—with confidence! (get an adult assistant to help if needed). Remember, this is tricky and will take some practice. Embrace whatever fun and funky shapes result.

Bake the pizza for 5 to 7 minutes, until there are dark brown bubbles around the crust. While it is baking, stretch and top the next pizza. When it is done, use your oven mitts to remove it carefully from the oven with a peel or a large spatula (get an adult assistant to help if needed). Let it cool on the cutting board for just a moment. Place the basil leaves on the pizza. Slice and serve immediately. Repeat with the remaining dough and toppings.

Store unused dough in a small round plastic container that will hold roughly 2 cups. Clean plastic pint containers for sour cream or yogurt work well.

**Toppings
(for a classic pizza)**

Tomato sauce (I just use good-quality crushed tomatoes, such as Bianco Denapoli, straight from the can)

Fresh mozzarella

Very good quality extra-virgin olive oil

Flaky sea salt

Fresh basil

Other topping ideas

corn kernels, cut off the cob; greens, such as dandelion or kale, cleaned and chopped; olives; cured meat such as prosciutto or soppressata

Serving suggestions
I like to wrap these rolls in
a clean linen and set a bowlful
on the table, so that people
can grab themselves a warm roll
when they're ready for it.

Dinner Rolls

Makes 12 rolls

Difficulty level Beginner

**Time from start of mixing
to baked bread** 4 hours
(plus 3 hours ahead to
prepare the sponge)

Baking vessel A large skillet
(alternatively a casserole
dish or sheet pan)

Mixer Needed

Ingredients

Sponge
(make 3 hours ahead)

½ cup (120 grams) warm
whole milk (about 85°F)

¼ teaspoon (1 gram) instant
dry yeast

⅔ cup (93 grams)
bread flour

Fluffy, light, yeasty, warm, tender dinner rolls are one of
life's most indulgent joys. These are a holiday staple in my
household, served warm on the table.

Parker House rolls from the *Joy of Cooking* book were one
of the first breads I learned how to bake with my mom.
These rolls take that same template for a fluffy soft roll
and add a little more flavor using the sponge method. The
double brushing of melted butter, both before and after
baking, takes these over the top.

I love to bake them in a skillet or enameled cast-iron dish
and then serve them straight from the oven. Any baking
sheet or pan will work, as long as they are positioned so
that they are just barely touching. They also make great
slider buns for leftover sandwiches (although we never
seem to have any leftover in my house).

To make the sponge

**Warm the milk until a drop on the wrist feels pleasantly
warm—about 85°F.** In a small bowl, combine the milk
and yeast and stir to dissolve. Add the flour and mix until
combined. Cover the bowl and set aside in a warm, draft-
free spot for about 3 hours, until it has doubled in size
and is very bubbly.

Continued ∿

Dough

1 cup (240 grams) warm
   whole milk (about 85°F)

½ teaspoon (2 grams)
   instant dry yeast

2 tablespoons (25 grams)
   granulated sugar

1 medium egg (60 grams),
   room temperature

1 tablespoon (9 grams)
   kosher salt

2 cups (179 grams) sponge

2⅔ cups (373 grams)
   bread flour

½ cup (113 grams) unsalted
   butter, melted, plus more
   for the skillet

⅓ cup (90 grams) unsalted
   butter, melted, for the
   skillet and brushing
   the rolls

To make the dough

In the bowl of a stand mixer, measure the warm milk and yeast. You can remove the bowl from the mixer and do this part by hand. Whisk to dissolve the yeast. Add the sugar and whisk it in. Add the egg and whisk to combine. Add the kosher salt and whisk to dissolve. Add the sponge and measure the flour into the bowl. Place the bowl back on the mixer, fitted with the dough hook attachment.

Mix for 3 minutes at medium speed. Check to make sure all the ingredients are combined well by scraping the bottom of the bowl with a spatula. Let rest for 3 minutes.

After 3 minutes, mix again on medium for 3 to 5 minutes, until the dough is cohesive and strong. Add the butter, 1 tablespoon at a time, mixing in between each addition, until all the butter is mixed in. Mix for about 3 more minutes after all the butter is incorporated, until the dough is smooth, supple, and shiny.

Remove the bowl from the mixer and scrape the sides of the bowl clean with your plastic dough scraper. Cover the bowl with a clean linen and let rest for 1 hour in a warm, draft-free spot.

After an hour, give the dough a turn. To do so, dampen your hand a bit. Loosen the edges of the dough from the bowl, using your damp hand and a damp plastic dough scraper. Lift up the edge of the dough farthest from you, grabbing a healthy pinch and stretching upward. Fold that handful over the top of the dough and press it down into the dough. Continue this stretching and folding, going around the dough until it has all been stretched and folded.

Let rest again for 30 minutes to 1 hour.

Prepare a skillet (or a baking dish or sheet pan) by buttering the bottom and sides.

After 30 minutes to an hour, the dough should have risen noticeably in the bowl. You should be able to see bubbles in the dough. If you can see the rising and the bubbles, it's time to divide the dough. If not, let it rest for 15 more minutes. Check the dough every 10 to 15 minutes and divide it when you see an increase in size and bubbles. When it's ready, use a dough scraper to scrape the dough out of the bowl and onto a very lightly floured work surface.

Divide the dough into 12 equal-size pieces (each should weigh about 80 grams.) Place each piece of dough on an unfloured work surface. Lightly flour your hands, then use the palm of your hand to gently press the dough against the surface. Move your hand in a circular motion, pressing very gently, using the spot where the dough is sticking as kind of an anchor. Round each piece until you are satisfied with the shape. You can lightly flour your hands as needed to keep the dough from sticking to you.

If you are unable to get a round shape that you are satisfied with, roll the dough piece between your hands (almost like playdough) until you get a ball.

Once each roll is rounded, place it in the skillet. All the rolls should be nestled next to each other, just barely touching. Cover with a clean linen and let rise in warm spot for 1 hour, or until they double in size.

While the rolls are rising, preheat the oven to 375°F and place a rack in the middle position (get an adult assistant to help if needed).

After an hour (or when they have doubled in size), brush the tops of the rolls with melted butter. (Hang onto any leftover butter—you'll brush them again when you take them out.) Using your oven mitts, place the skillet carefully in the oven (get an adult assistant to help if needed). Close the door and set a timer for 15 minutes.

After 15 minutes, check to see if the rolls are baking evenly. If not, use your oven mitts to rotate the skillet (get an adult assistant to help if needed). Bake for 5 to 10 minutes longer, or until the buns are golden brown.

Once the rolls are baked, use your oven mitts to remove the skillet carefully from the oven (get an adult assistant to help if needed). Place it on a heatproof surface (such as the stovetop) and brush the tops with melted butter again. Let cool for 5 minutes, then carefully remove the rolls from the skillet using a spatula. Serve immediately (or as soon as possible.)

Pita

Makes 10 pitas

Difficulty level Beginner

Time from start of mixing to baked bread 5 hours

Baking vessel Baking steel or stone

This is an easy dough to put together and makes delicious pita or flatbreads. I love to use these to scoop up hummus and olive oil, but they can also be used to make pita sandwiches, stuffed with yogurt, cucumbers, sprouts, tomatoes, and whatever else you can imagine.

There are two keys to getting pita to puff up and form that distinctive pocket. The first is that the gluten needs to relax all the way before you bake them. You'll need to let them rest for at least 30 minutes after you shape them and before you bake them. The second is that they need to hit a very hot surface and bake quickly. The best way to do this at home is to preheat a cast-iron skillet, baking stone, or baking steel thoroughly. I'm going to give you directions here for baking in the oven on a stone or a steel, but if you like, you can try baking them in a cast-iron skillet on the stovetop. (You can refer to the instructions for making tortillas on page 101.) Even if you don't quite get the gluten relaxed enough or the baking surface hot enough, pita that don't puff make great flatbreads.

I almost always rest this dough overnight by putting it in the fridge about an hour after mixing and taking it out about an hour before shaping. That allows the flavor and texture of the wheat to mellow and develop and makes a more tender and flavorful pita. That's not necessary, however, and if you're looking for a quick dough to make same day, this one will give you great results in a relatively short period of time (for bread, that is).

Continued ⌇

These are good for pita pocket sandwiches with raita, sprouts, and chopped tomato; scooping up hummus, olive oil, or any other dip.

Ingredients

1½ cups (354 grams) warm water (about 85°F)

1½ cups (367 grams) unstrained whole-milk, plain yogurt (not Greek)

1 teaspoon (4 grams) instant dry yeast

½ cup (108 grams) extra-virgin olive oil

2 tablespoons (18 grams) kosher salt

3½ cups (490 grams) bread flour

3½ cups (490 grams) whole wheat flour

In a medium bowl, whisk together the warm water, yogurt, and yeast thoroughly. Add the olive oil and salt and whisk to combine. Add the flours and mix together with your hand until all the ingredients are combined. Let rest for 3 minutes.

After 3 minutes, wet your hand and mix the dough well in the bowl for about 5 minutes, lifting, stretching, folding, and pressing it down. Mix in this way until the dough is smooth, stretchy, and strong. Alternatively, mix the dough in the bowl of a stand mixer fitted with the dough hook on medium for about 5 minutes.

Scrape any dough off your fingers and the edges of the bowl back onto the dough—it will heal itself like magic and become part of the dough again!

Cover the bowl with a clean linen and place in a warm, draft-free spot to rise. Let it rest for 30 minutes to allow the gluten to relax.

After 30 minutes, fold the dough. This will even out the temperature, re-distribute areas of more activity, and strengthen the gluten. To do so, loosen it from the edges of the bowl. Lift the side of the dough up, stretch it over the top, and press it back down into the bowl. Do this a few times until you have lifted, stretched, and folded all the dough.

For more tender and flavorful pita, refrigerate the dough overnight or up to 48 hours at this point. Remove the dough from the fridge and let come to room temperature (it usually takes about an hour) before you move on to the next step. For same-day results, continue with the next steps.

Cover it again and let it rest for 30 minutes.

After 30 minutes, fold the dough one more time.

Cover it again and let it rest for 30 minutes to 1 hour. After this last rest, it should have risen noticeably in the bowl. You should be able to see bubbles in the dough. If you can see the rising and the bubbles, it's time to divide the dough. If not, let it rest for 15 more minutes. Check the dough every 10 to 15 minutes and divide it when you see a dramatic increase in size and lots of bubbles.

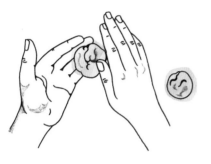

Once it has risen, it is ready to divide and shape into balls. Scoop the dough out of the bowl onto a clean work surface and divide the dough into 10 equal-size pieces. You can use a little flour on your hands, if you need, to keep the dough from sticking, but try to keep the flour minimal.

Place one ball on a clean, unfloured work surface in front of you. Cup your hands around it and roll the dough in a circular motion, making as round and even a ball of dough as you can. Repeat this with all the dough pieces. Let them rest for 20 minutes.

While the dough is resting, insert a baking stone or steel in the oven on a rack in the middle position and preheat to 500°F (get an adult assistant for help if needed).

After 20 minutes, flatten each dough ball into a disk ¼ inch thick and about 6 inches in diameter. You can use as much flour as you need on your hands and your work surface to keep the dough from sticking. Let them rest for 30 minutes.

After 30 minutes, you're ready to bake. Lightly dust each pita with flour so that they slide onto the baking surface easily. Bake them one or two at a time, using oven mitts and a metal spatula or a baguette peel to slide them onto the baking surface (get an adult assistant for help if needed).

Bake for 1 minute. The pitas should puff up and be lightly brown on the bottom. Flip them over, wearing oven mitts and using a metal spatula or tongs, and bake for another minute, until the (now) bottom has lightly browned.

Once they are lightly browned on both sides, remove them carefully with a metal spatula or tongs and set them on a plate (get an adult assistant for help if needed). Cover them with a clean linen to make sure they retain some steam and heat. Repeat with the remaining pita dough pieces.

These are best served warm. If you want to keep them for a day, seal them up as tightly as possible so they stay soft. To reheat, use a clean spray bottle to spritz them lightly with water and heat quickly in a hot oven.

Flour Tortillas

Makes Twelve 6-inch
(taco-size) flour tortillas

Difficulty level Beginner

**Time from start of mixing
to baked bread** 3 hours

Baking vessel Skillet,
griddle, or comal
(a heavy, flat griddle
used in Mexico)

Mixer Optional

Quesadilla was one of my first words. It's still one of my favorite things to eat, and taco night is a weekly occasion in our home—at a minimum. While I also love masa tortillas, made with corn, I am a huge fan of a soft, tender flour tortilla. For a while, my kids didn't realize the difference between the words *flour* and *flower* and started calling these bumblebee tortillas because they associated bumblebees with flowers and thought I was offering them "flower" tortillas. The name stuck, and we still call these bumblebee tortillas at our table.

In northern Mexico, these tortillas are often made with local Sonora wheat, which is a very low-protein, soft white wheat. I use pastry flour here, which will give you a similarly very soft and tender tortilla. If you're able to find Sonora wheat flour, that will make the ideal tortilla.

These are best eaten very fresh. If you want to prepare them ahead of time, you can make the dough, rest it, and then shape the tortillas so that they are all rolled out and ready to griddle. Then hold them in the fridge and griddle them right before you want to eat them.

Ingredients

2½ cups (350 grams)
pastry flour

½ cup (102 grams) cold lard
or vegetable shortening

1 tablespoon (9 grams)
kosher salt

¾ cup (177 grams)
ice-cold water

Measure the flour into a medium mixing bowl. Measure the lard directly into the flour. Use your fingers to rub the lard into the flour until the mixture is crumbly and there are no pieces of lard bigger than a pea.

Dissolve the salt in the cold water.

Pour the water and salt mixture into the flour and lard mixture. Stir very well with a spoon or your hand until all the ingredients are combined. Knead the dough by hand (or you can use a mixer with the dough hook attachment)

Continued 〜

in the bowl for a minute or so, just until the dough holds together. Remove the dough from the bowl and wrap it in plastic wrap. Allow to chill in the fridge for at least 2 hours or up to 2 days.

After the dough has chilled, remove it from the fridge and unwrap it. Divide the dough into 12 equal balls, each about the size of a small apricot. Roll the balls between your palms until they are evenly round.

Next, on a very lightly floured work surface, use a rolling pin to flatten each ball into a thin tortilla about 6 inches in diameter. If you have a tortilla press, you can use it to flatten the balls, but you'll probably want to finish them with a rolling pin anyway—these are nicest when they are pretty thin. As you roll each tortilla flat, place it on a sheet of parchment or waxed paper. Layer the tortillas between sheets of paper so that they are flat and not touching. Use as many pieces of paper as you need until they are all rolled out.

Preheat a cast-iron skillet, griddle, or comal over medium-high heat (if you're using a cast-iron skillet, you may want to smear some vegetable oil very lightly on it before preheating). The baking surface needs to be plenty hot, so make sure to give it a few minutes to preheat.

Griddle the tortillas one at a time for about 60 seconds on each side, until both sides have golden-brown blisters. Use tongs or a spatula to flip them (get an adult assistant for help if needed). The tortillas may puff up a little as they cook, but they will flatten as they cool. Keep the finished tortillas in a covered dish or wrap them in a towel to keep them warm while you work.

These are best served right away. If you do have some left over, you can store them in an airtight container for a few days and quickly reheat them in a hot skillet before serving. They are perfect for tacos, taquitos, or bite-size quesadillas.

Oat Bread

Makes Two 8½ by 4½-inch loaves

Difficulty level Beginner

Time from start of mixing to baked bread 6 hours (plus 3 hours ahead to prepare the sponge)

Baking vessel Two 8½ by 4½-inch bread pans

Mixer Optional

Ingredients

Sponge (make 3 hours ahead)

¾ cup (177 grams) warm water

½ teaspoon (2 grams) instant dry yeast

¾ cup (105 grams) bread flour

¾ cup (105 grams) whole wheat flour

Oatmeal (make about 30 minutes ahead)

½ cup (50 grams) rolled oats

1 cup (236 grams) cold tap water

This bread is very similar to the honey whole wheat bread (page 49), with the addition of cooked oats—aka oatmeal. The cooked oats in this formula have an effect similar to the cooked milk and flour in the milk bread recipe on page 57. Cooking the oats gelatinizes the starches, which give creaminess and longevity to your bread. The oats also add some good nutrition.

The bakers at Tartine make a similar bread, adding cooked grains to the classic country bread, and it has always been one of my favorites.

To make the sponge

Pour the warm water into a medium mixing bowl—make sure there is plenty of room in it for the sponge to grow. Sprinkle the yeast on top. Stir with a spoon to dissolve the yeast in the water. Add both flours to the bowl. Stir with a wooden spoon or your hand until the flour and water are combined well and there are no lumps. Cover the mixing bowl with a clean dish towel and let rest on the countertop in a warm, draft-free spot for 3 hours. It's ready to use when it has doubled in size and is very bubbly.

About 30 minutes before you are ready to mix the dough, prepare the oatmeal. To do so, stir together the rolled oats and cold water in a medium saucepan. Cook over medium-low heat until all the water is absorbed and the oatmeal is creamy. Set aside to cool.

Continued ∿

103

Dough

1⅓ cups (314 grams) warm water (about 85°F)

½ teaspoon (2 grams) instant dry yeast

4½ cups (409 grams) sponge

2 tablespoons (42 grams) honey

1 tablespoon + 1 teaspoon (12 grams) kosher salt

1½ cups (210 grams) whole wheat flour

1½ cups (210 grams) bread flour

1½ cups (205 grams) cooked oat porridge

2 tablespoons neutral oil, for greasing the pans

2 tablespoons milk for brushing the tops of the loaves

¼ cup rolled oats for sprinkling over the tops of the loaves

To make the dough

In a large mixing bowl, combine the warm water, yeast, sponge, and honey. Stir with your hand or a wooden spoon to combine (the sponge doesn't need to dissolve completely, just be broken up a bit). Add the salt and stir to dissolve.

Add the whole wheat and the bread flours to the wet ingredients in the bowl and stir with your hand until there is no more dry flour. Let the dough rest for 3 minutes so the flour can begin to absorb the water and the gluten can start to form.

After 3 minutes, add the porridge and finish mixing. Wet your hand and mix the dough in the bowl for about 5 minutes, squeezing to make sure everything is well combined and then lifting, stretching, folding, and pressing it down. Mix in this way until the dough is smooth, stretchy, and strong. It should still feel a little bit sticky. Alternatively, mix the dough in the bowl of a stand mixer fitted with the dough hook on low for about 5 minutes.

Scrape any dough off your fingers and the edges of the bowl back onto the dough—it will heal itself like magic and become part of the dough again!

Cover the bowl with a clean linen and place in a warm, draft-free spot to rise. Let it rest for 30 minutes to allow the gluten to relax.

After 30 minutes, fold the dough. This will even out the temperature, re-distribute areas of more activity, and strengthen the gluten. To do so, loosen it from the edges of the bowl. Lift the side of the dough up, stretch it over the top, and press it back down into the bowl. Do this a few times until you have lifted, stretched, and folded all the dough.

Cover it again and let it rest for 30 minutes.

After 30 minutes, fold the dough one more time.

Cover it again and let it rest for 30 minutes to 1 hour. After this last rest, it should have risen noticeably in the bowl. You should be able to see bubbles in the edges or top of the

Mixing

1. Combine wet and dry ingredients

2. Squeeze and pinch until dough comes together

3. Stretch and fold well to develop a strong, elastic dough

dough. If you can see the rising and the bubbles, it's time to divide the dough. If not, let it rest for 15 more minutes. Check the dough every 10 to 15 minutes and divide it when you see a dramatic increase in size and lots of bubbles.

While it's finishing rising in the bowl, get two 8½ by 4½-inch rectangular bread pans ready by lightly oiling the sides. Use a pastry brush to spread the oil evenly all over the inside of the pans.

To divide the dough, scoop it out of the bowl (a bowl scraper is handy for this, but you can also use a spatula or just your fingers). Divide the dough equally in half using your bench knife to gently cut it. If you are using a scale, each half should weigh about 700 grams.

To shape the loaves, pat each portion of the dough gently into a rectangle, roughly 12 by 6 inches. The shorter sides of the rectangle should be at the top and bottom and the longer sides should be on the right and left sides. Shape one loaf at a time. Using your fingertips, roll the top edge toward you, almost as if you're rolling up a carpet. Press the rolled part gently into the flat part as you continue to roll it toward you. Once it's all rolled up, press the seam together where the bottom edge meets the rolled-up part of the loaf. Place the shaped loaf into the pan with the seam on the bottom. Repeat with the second loaf.

Preheat the oven to 400°F and place a rack in the middle position (get an adult assistant to help if needed).

Cover the loaves loosely with a clean linen and place in a warm, draft-free spot.

Let the loaves rise for 30 minutes to an hour, until they have risen taller than the loaf pans. If you poke a loaf gently with your fingertips, it should feel full of air and spring back slowly. Wait until they have risen noticeably in the pan before you bake them, even if it takes more than an hour. Once they have risen in the pan (the final proofing), you're ready to bake.

Continued ∾

Using a clean pastry brush, brush the tops of the loaves with the milk so that they are evenly coated. Sprinkle some rolled oats over the milk—they will stick and toast nicely as the loaf bakes.

Next, score the loaves (for more about scoring, see page 159). Use some sharp kitchen scissors (get an adult assistant to help if needed) to snip the top six to eight times. Alternatively, use a sharp knife to make small slits or slashes in the top of each loaf.

Once the loaves have been brushed with milk, sprinkled with oats, and scored, you are ready to put them in the oven. Place the pan gently on the rack in the middle of the oven (get an adult assistant to help if needed). Close the oven door and set a timer for 20 minutes.

After 20 minutes, take a peek at your loaves. If either looks like it is darker on one side, use oven mitts to turn the pans half a turn so that they will finish baking evenly (get an adult assistant to help if needed).

Bake for 10 to 15 more minutes. The loaves are finished baking when they are an even medium brown all over the top. If they look speckled or blonde, give them a few more minutes. Remember, your oven may run a little hot. If they are well browned on top, go ahead and take them out.

When they are done baking, use oven mitts to remove the pans from the oven (get an adult assistant to help if needed.) Set the pan on a heatproof surface (such as a stovetop) to cool for 10 minutes.

After 10 minutes, gently remove the loaves from the pans (get an adult assistant to help if needed). Set the loaf on a cooling rack and let cool for at least 1 hour.

You can keep your bread in a bread box or bag on the countertop for up to 4 days. If it starts to feel stale, you can toast the slices. To store it for longer, slice it and keep it in a sealed container in the freezer. To serve, take as many slices as you'd like from the freezer and toast them.

This bread is great for thick-sliced toast and sandwiches. It is my favorite for avocado toast and open-faced almond butter and honey sandwiches.

This bread is good for sandwiches (roast beef and grilled cheese are favorites) or toast with cream cheese and jam.

Rye Loaf

Makes Two 8½ by 4½-inch loaves

Difficulty level Beginner

Time from start of mixing to baked bread 6 hours (plus 3 hours ahead to prepare the sponge)

Baking vessel Two 8½ by 4½-inch loaf pans

Ingredients

Rye Sponge (make 3 hours ahead)

1¼ cups (295 grams) cool water (about 70°F)

½ teaspoon (2 grams) instant dry yeast

2¼ cups (293 grams) pumpernickel rye flour

Pumpernickel was always my favorite bagel flavor when I was a kid. I think I learned to love dark, hearty, earthy rye breads while living in Germany. Rye isn't always thought of as a kids' flavor, but I loved it and now my kids love it. I heartily urge you to give it a try. It has a mellow malty sweetness that is really a treat.

This bread is great for savory sandwiches, like ham and cheese, but I also really love it with sweet things. A favorite way to eat it is inspired by one of my favorite ways to dress a bagel—toasted and topped with cream cheese and jam. Blackberry jam is a particular favorite.

To make the sponge

In a medium mixing bowl, measure the water. Sprinkle the yeast on top of the water and stir with a spoon to dissolve the yeast. Add the flour to the bowl. Stir with a wooden spoon or your hand until the flour and water are combined and there are no lumps. Cover the mixing bowl with a clean linen and let rest on the countertop for about 3 hours. It's ready to use when it has doubled in size and is very bubbly.

Continued 〜

Dough

1½ cups (354 grams) warm
water (about 85°F)

½ teaspoon (2 grams)
instant dry yeast

2 tablespoons (28 grams)
raw sugar

1 tablespoon (21 grams)
blackstrap molasses

1 tablespoon + 1 teaspoon
(12 grams) kosher salt

6⅓ cups (495 grams)
rye sponge

1¾ cups (245 grams)
bread flour

1 cup (130 grams)
pumpernickel rye flour

¾ cup (98 grams) whole
wheat flour

2 tablespoons neutral oil
for the bread pans

Water for brushing
the loaves

To make the dough

In a large mixing bowl, measure the warm water, yeast, raw sugar, molasses, and salt. Stir to dissolve the sugar. Add the sponge and stir to disperse. Add the flours and mix to combine all the ingredients. Let rest for 3 minutes.

After 3 minutes, wet your hand and mix the dough well in the bowl for about 5 minutes, squeezing to make sure everything is well combined and then lifting, stretching, folding, and pressing it down. Mix in this way until the dough is smooth, stretchy, and strong. It should still feel a little bit sticky. Alternatively, mix the dough in the bowl of a stand mixer fitted with the dough hook on medium for about 5 minutes.

Scrape any dough off your fingers and the edges of the bowl back onto the dough—it will heal itself like magic and become part of the dough again!

Cover the bowl with a clean linen and place in a warm, draft-free spot to rise. Let it rest for 30 minutes to allow the gluten to relax.

After 30 minutes, fold the dough. This will even out the temperature, re-distribute areas of more activity, and strengthen the gluten. To do so, loosen it from the edges of the bowl. Lift the side of the dough up, stretch it over the top, and press it back down into the bowl. Do this a few times until you have lifted, stretched, and folded all the dough.

Cover it again and let it rest for 30 minutes.

After 30 minutes, fold the dough one more time.

Cover it again and let it rest for 30 minutes to 1 hour. After this last rest, it should have risen noticeably in the bowl. You should be able to see bubbles at the edges or top of the dough. If you can see the rising and the bubbles, it's time to divide the dough. If not, let it rest for 15 more minutes. Check the dough every 10 to 15 minutes and divide it when you see a dramatic increase in size and lots of bubbles.

While it's finishing rising in the bowl, get two 8½ by 4½-inch rectangular bread pans ready by lightly oiling the sides. Use your fingers or a pastry brush to spread the oil evenly all over the inside of the pans.

Once it has doubled in size, scoop the dough out of the bowl onto a clean work surface.

To divide the dough, scoop it out of the bowl (a bowl scraper is handy for this, but you can also use a spatula or just your fingers). Divide the dough equally in half using your bench knife to gently cut it. If you are using a scale, each half should weigh about 700 grams.

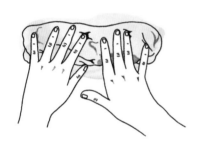

To shape the loaves, pat each portion of the dough gently into a rectangle, roughly 12 by 6 inches. The shorter sides of the rectangle should be at the top and bottom, and the longer sides should be on the right- and left-hand sides. Shape one loaf at a time. Using your fingertips, roll the top edge toward you, almost as if you're rolling up a carpet. Press the rolled part gently into the flat part as you continue to roll it toward you. Once it's all rolled up, press the seam together where the bottom edge meets the rolled-up part of the loaf. Place the shaped loaf into the pan with the seam on the bottom. Repeat with the second loaf.

Preheat the oven to 400°F and place a rack in the middle position (get an adult assistant to help if needed).

Let the loaves rise for 30 minutes to 1 hour, until they have risen taller than the loaf pans. If you poke a loaf gently with your fingertips, it should feel full of air and spring back slowly. Wait until they have risen noticeably in the pan before you bake them, even if it takes more than an hour. Once they have risen in the pan (the final proofing), you're ready to bake.

Using a clean pastry brush, brush the tops of the loaves with water so that they are evenly coated. If desired, sprinkle lightly with flour for a dramatic contrast to the darker dough.

Continued ⌣

Next, score the loaves (for more about scoring, see page 159). Use some sharp kitchen scissors (get an adult assistant to help if needed) to snip the top six to eight times. Alternatively, use a sharp knife to make small slits or slashes in the top of each loaf.

Once the loaves have been brushed with water and scored, you are ready to put them in the oven. Place the pan gently on the rack in the middle of the oven (get an adult assistant to help if needed). Close the oven door and set a timer for 20 minutes.

After 20 minutes, take a peek at your loaves. If either looks like it is darker on one side, use oven mitts to turn the pans half a turn so that they will finish baking evenly (get an adult assistant to help if needed).

Bake for 10 to 15 more minutes. The loaves are finished baking when they are an even medium brown all over the top. If they looks speckled or blonde, give them a few more minutes. Remember, your oven may run a little hot. If they are well browned on top, go ahead and take them out.

When they are done baking, use oven mitts to remove the pans from the oven (get an adult assistant to help if needed.) Set the pan on a heatproof surface (such as a stovetop) to cool for 10 minutes.

After 10 minutes, gently remove the loaves from the pans (get an adult assistant to help if needed). Set the loaf on a cooling rack and let cool for at least 1 hour.

You can keep your bread in a bread box or bag on the countertop for up to 4 days. If it starts to feel stale, you can cut slices and toast them. To store it for longer, slice it and keep it in a sealed container in the freezer. To serve, take as many slices as you'd like from the freezer and toast them.

Semolina Bread

Makes Two 8½ by 4½-inch loaves

Difficulty level Beginner

Time from start of mixing to baked bread 6 hours (plus 3 hours ahead to prepare the sponge)

Baking vessel Two 8½ by 4½-inch bread pans

Ingredients

Sponge (make 3 hours ahead)

1 cup (236 grams) warm water (about 85°F)

½ teaspoon (2 grams) instant dry yeast

¾ cup (105 grams) bread flour

¾ cup (105 grams) whole wheat flour

Semolina is the name for medium-coarse ground durum wheat. Durum is an amber-colored wheat that is very high in protein and is harder than other wheat berries (the word *durum* actually means "hard" in Latin and is the root of the word *durable*). That makes it a little more difficult to mill finely enough to make a soft flour. Because of this, durum was often milled very coarsely, resulting in what we call "semolina." With modern technology it is possible to mill durum flour more finely, but semolina is still very common. Semolina is most often used to make pasta or couscous, but it also makes a lovely, toothy, flavorful bread.

To make the sponge

In a medium mixing bowl—make sure there is plenty of room in it for the sponge to get dramatically bigger— pour the water. Sprinkle the yeast on top of the water. Stir with a spoon to dissolve the yeast in the water. Add both flours to the bowl. Stir with a wooden spoon or your hand until the flour and water are combined well and there are no lumps. Cover the mixing bowl with a clean linen and let rest on the countertop in a warm, draft-free spot for 3 hours. It's ready to use when it has doubled in size and is very bubbly.

Continued ∿

Dough

2 cups (472 grams) warm water (about 85°F)

½ teaspoon (2 grams) instant dry yeast

1 tablespoon + 1 teaspoon (12 grams) kosher salt

5 cups (308 grams) sponge

4 cups (640 grams) semolina flour

¼ cup all-purpose flour for dusting the tops

Olive oil or other neutral oil for coating the pans

To make the dough

In a large mixing bowl, measure the warm water. Measure the yeast in and stir to dissolve. Measure the salt in and stir to dissolve. Add the sponge and the 4 cups semolina flour. Use your hand to squeeze and stir the ingredients together until they form a dough. Alternatively, mix in a stand mixer fitted with the dough hook on low for 3 minutes. Let it rest for 3 minutes.

After 3 minutes, wet your hand and mix the dough thoroughly in the bowl for about 5 minutes, squeezing to make sure everything is well combined and then lifting, stretching, folding, and pressing it down. Mix in this way until the dough is smooth, stretchy, and strong. Alternatively, mix the dough in the bowl of a stand mixer fitted with the dough hook on medium for about 5 minutes.

Scrape any dough off your fingers and the edges of the bowl back onto the dough—it will heal itself like magic and become part of the dough again!

Cover the bowl with a clean linen and place in a warm, draft-free spot to rise. Let it rest for 30 minutes to allow the gluten to relax.

After 30 minutes, fold the dough. This will even out the temperature, re-distribute areas of more activity, and strengthen the gluten. To do so, loosen it from the edges of the bowl. Lift the side of the dough up, stretch it over the top, and press it back down into the bowl. Do this a few times until you have lifted, stretched, and folded all the dough.

Cover it again and let it rest for 30 minutes.

After 30 minutes, fold the dough one more time.

Cover it again and let it rest for 30 minutes to 1 hour. After this last rest, it should have risen noticeably in the bowl. You should be able to see bubbles in the dough and at the edges or top of the dough. If you can see the rising and the bubbles, it's time to divide the dough. If not, let it rest for 15 more minutes. Check the dough every 10 to 15 minutes and divide it when you see a dramatic increase in size and lots of bubbles.

While it's finishing rising in the bowl, get two 8½ by 4½-inch rectangular bread pans ready by lightly greasing the sides. Use a clean brush to coat them in olive oil or another neutral oil.

To divide the dough, scoop it out of the bowl (a bowl scraper is handy for this, but you can also use a spatula or just your fingers). Divide the dough equally in half using your bench knife to gently cut it. If you are using a scale, each half should weigh about 700 grams.

To shape the loaves, pat each portion of the dough gently into a rectangle, roughly 12 by 6 inches. The shorter sides of the rectangle should be at the top and bottom, and the longer sides should be on the right and left sides. Shape one loaf at a time. Using your fingertips, roll the top edge toward you, almost as if you're rolling up a carpet. Press the rolled part gently into the flat part as you continue to roll it toward you.

Once it's all rolled up, press the seam together where the bottom edge meets the rolled-up part of the loaf. Place the shaped loaf into the pan with the seam on the bottom. Repeat with the second loaf.

Preheat the oven to 400°F and place a rack in the middle position (get an adult assistant to help if needed).

Cover the loaves loosely with a clean, dry linen and place in a warm, draft-free spot.

Let the loaves rise for 30 minutes to an hour, until they have risen taller than the loaf pans. If you poke a loaf gently with your fingertips, it should feel full of air and spring back slowly. Wait until they have risen noticeably in the pan before you bake them, even if it takes more than an hour. Once they have risen in the pan (the final proofing), you're ready to bake.

Once the loaves have risen in the pan and are ready to bake, lightly dust the tops with the all-purpose flour. To do so, get a fine-mesh sieve or a sifter. Place the flour in the sieve and shake it over each loaf until it is lightly coated. (You can place it in a sheet pan or over parchment to catch loose flour if you like.)

Continued ⌇

Next, score the loaves (for more about scoring, see page 159). Use some sharp kitchen scissors to snip the top six to eight times (get an adult assistant to help if needed). Alternatively, use a sharp knife to make small slits or slashes in the top of each loaf.

Once the loaves have been dusted with flour and scored, you are ready to put them in the oven. Place the pan gently on the rack in the middle of the oven (get an adult assistant to help if needed). Close the oven door and set a timer for 20 minutes.

After 20 minutes, take a peek at your loaves. If either looks like it is darker on one side, use oven mitts to turn the pans half a turn so that they will finish baking evenly (get an adult assistant to help if needed).

Bake for 10 to 15 more minutes. The loaves are finished baking when they have browned around the edges (where they're not dusted with flour.) If they look speckled or blonde at the edges, give them a few more minutes. Remember, your oven may run a little hot. If they look done, go ahead and take them out.

When they are done baking, use oven mitts to remove the pans from the oven (get an adult assistant to help if needed.) Set the pan on a heatproof surface (such as a stovetop) to cool for 10 minutes.

After 10 minutes, gently remove the loaves from the pans (get an adult assistant to help if needed). Set the loaf on a cooling rack and let cool for at least 1 hour.

You can keep your bread in a bread box or bag on the countertop for up to 4 days. If it starts to feel stale, you can cut slices and toast them. To store it for longer, slice it and keep it in a sealed container in the freezer. To serve, take as many slices as you'd like from the freezer and toast them.

This bread is good for toast, French toast, sandwiches, and bread crumbs.

This bread is good for toast, French toast, and sandwiches.

Graham Bread

Makes Two 8½ by 4½ inch pan loaves

Difficulty level
Intermediate

Time from start of mixing to baked bread 6 hours (plus 3 hours ahead to prepare the sponge)

Baking vessel Two 8½ by 4½-inch loaf pans

Ingredients

**Sponge
(make 3 hours ahead)**

¾ cup (177 grams) warm water (about 85°F)

½ teaspoon (2 grams) instant dry yeast

⅔ cup (93 grams) bread flour

⅔ cup (93 grams) graham flour

Graham flour is whole wheat flour that hasn't been sifted at all. The best way to get graham flour is to buy it straight from a mill or to mill it yourself. Most commercial whole wheat flour is sifted into its constituent parts and then reassembled without the germ and oils, which are the more perishable parts of the wheat berry. So, strictly speaking, most "whole wheat flour" isn't actually whole!

It's actually pretty easy to mill your own graham flour. There are many ways to do it at home (see page 121). You can put the wheat berries in a food processor, a high-powered blender (like a VitaMix), a mill attachment to a KitchenAid mixer, a burr-grinder coffee mill, a spice grinder, or a tabletop mill. I have a fantastic KoMo countertop mill that makes gorgeous home-milled whole grain flour, but we've also milled wheat berries at my kids' school with a $30 spice grinder with great success.

To make the sponge

In a medium mixing bowl, measure the warm water. Sprinkle the yeast on top of the water and stir it with a spoon to dissolve the yeast. Add both flours to the bowl. Stir with a wooden spoon or your hand until the flour and water are combined well and there are no lumps. Cover the mixing bowl with a clean linen and let rest on the countertop in a warm, draft-free spot for 3 hours. It's ready to use when it has doubled in size and is very bubbly.

Continued ∿

Dough

2 cups (480 grams)
   whole milk, warmed
   to about 85°F

1 tablespoon (21 grams)
   blackstrap molasses

1 tablespoon (9 grams)
   kosher salt

4 cups (292 grams) sponge

2 cups (280 grams)
   graham flour

2 cups (280 grams)
   bread flour

¼ cup (57 grams)
   unsalted butter, room
   temperature, plus
   2 tablespoons for
   coating the bread pans

Milk for brushing

To make the dough

In a large mixing bowl, measure the warm milk, molasses, and salt. Stir to dissolve, then add the sponge and stir to disperse it a little.

Add the graham and the bread flours to the wet ingredients in the bowl and stir until there is no more dry flour. Let the dough rest for 3 minutes so the flour can begin to absorb the liquids and the gluten can start to form.

After 3 minutes, wet your hand and mix the dough in the bowl for about 5 minutes, squeezing to make sure everything is well combined and then lifting, stretching, folding, and pressing it down. Add the room temperature butter and mix for about 3 minutes more, until all the butter is incorporated into the dough. Mix in this way until the dough is smooth, stretchy, and strong. It should still feel a little bit sticky. Alternatively, mix the dough in the bowl of a stand mixer fitted with the dough hook on medium for about 5 minutes.

Cover the bowl with a clean linen and place in a warm, draft-free spot to rise. Let it rest for 30 minutes to allow the gluten to relax.

After 30 minutes, fold the dough. This will even out the temperature, re-distribute areas of more activity, and strengthen the gluten. To do so, loosen it from the edges of the bowl. Lift the side of the dough up, stretch it over the top, and press it back down into the bowl. Do this a few times until you have lifted, stretched, and folded all the dough.

Cover it again and let it rest for 30 minutes.

After 30 minutes, fold the dough one more time.

Cover it again and let it rest for 30 minutes to 1 hour. After this last rest, it should have risen noticeably in the bowl. You should be able to see bubbles in the dough and at the edges or top of the dough. If you can see the rising and the bubbles, it's time to divide the dough. If not, let it rest for 15 more minutes. Check the dough every 10 to 15 minutes and divide it when you see a dramatic increase in size and lots of bubbles.

Milling your own graham flour

These directions are for using a spice grinder, because I think that's the thing most people are likely to have, but the same instructions will work for a food processor. If you have a home mill, just follow the instructions that come with the mill.

Wheat berries can be obtained from bulk bins in health food–focused grocery stores or from a farm directly. You can also grow your own wheat if you have a little space. When the berries are fat and ready to be harvested, let them dry in the sun for a few weeks and separate them from the chaff before milling.

To mill the flour: Measure about 500 grams of wheat berries (you'll lose a little to the milling process, so you want to start with more than you need).

Place about 1 cup of the wheat berries (200 grams) in the spice grinder. Place the lid on the grinder and start grinding.

Continue until the wheat berries have been pulverized to a fine flour. Pour the flour out of the grinder and into bowl and repeat with the rest of the berries until all the berries are ground into flour. Use the flour immediately after milling (make sure to stick your nose in it as it comes out of the mill—the smell is incredible) or store in the fridge for up to a week.

While it's finishing rising in the bowl, get two 8½ by 4½-inch rectangular bread pans ready by lightly buttering the sides. Use your fingers or a pastry brush to spread the soft butter evenly all over the inside of the pans. Alternatively, brush with neutral oil.

Continued ∿

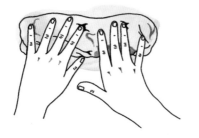

To divide the dough, scoop it out of the bowl (a bowl scraper is handy for this, but you can also use a spatula or just your fingers). Divide the dough equally in half using your bench knife to gently cut it. If you are using a scale, each half should weigh about 700 grams.

To shape the loaves, pat each portion of the dough gently into a rectangle, roughly 12 by 6 inches. The shorter sides of the rectangle should be at the top and bottom, and the longer sides should be on the right and left sides. Shape one loaf at a time. Using your fingertips, roll the top edge toward you, almost as if you're rolling up a carpet. Press the rolled part gently into the flat part as you continue to roll it toward you. Once it's all rolled up, press the seam together where the bottom edge meets the rolled-up part of the loaf. Place the shaped loaf into the pan with the seam on the bottom. Repeat with the second loaf.

Preheat the oven to 400°F and place a rack in the middle position (get an adult assistant to help if needed).

Cover the loaves loosely with a clean linen and place in a warm, draft-free spot.

Let the loaves rise for 30 minutes to 1 hour, until they have risen taller than the loaf pans. If you poke a loaf gently with your fingertip, it should feel full of air and spring back slowly. Wait until they have risen noticeably in the pan before you bake them, even if it takes more than an hour. Once they have risen in the pan (the final proofing), you're ready to bake.

Using a clean pastry brush, brush the tops of the loaves with milk so that they are evenly coated.

Next, score the loaves (for more about scoring, see page 159). Use some sharp kitchen scissors to snip the top six to eight times (get an adult assistant to help if needed). Alternatively, use a sharp knife to make small slits or slashes in the top of each loaf.

Baking

1. Brushing the top of the loaf with milk

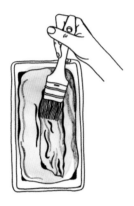

2. Snipping and/or scoring

Once the loaves have been brushed with milk and scored, you are ready to put them in the oven. Place the pan gently on the rack in the middle of the oven (get an adult assistant to help if needed). Close the oven door and set a timer for 20 minutes.

After 20 minutes, take a peek at your loaves. If either looks like it is darker on one side, use oven mitts to turn the pans half a turn so that they will finish baking evenly (get an adult assistant to help if needed).

Bake for 10 to 15 more minutes. The loaves are finished baking when they are an even medium brown all over the top. If they look speckled or blonde, give them a few more minutes. Remember, your oven may run a little hot. If they are well browned on top, go ahead and take them out.

When they are done baking, use oven mitts to remove the pans from the oven (get an adult assistant to help if needed.) Set the pan on a heatproof surface (such as a stovetop) to cool for 10 minutes.

After 10 minutes, gently remove the loaves from the pans (get an adult assistant to help if needed). Set the loaf on a cooling rack and let cool for at least 1 hour.

You can keep your bread in a bread box or bag on the countertop for up to 4 days. If it starts to feel stale, you can cut slices and toast them. To store it for longer, slice it and keep it in a sealed container in the freezer. To serve, take as many slices as you'd like from the freezer and toast them.

This bread is good served alongside any braised, saucy meats or with field peas and greens.

Cornbread

Makes One 8-inch round loaf

Difficulty level Beginner

Time from start of mixing to baked bread 1 hour

Baking vessel An 8-inch cast-iron skillet

I love cornbread anytime of the year, but my family always makes this cornbread on New Year's Day to go with black-eyed peas and greens for luck in the New Year.

This is only recipe in this book that's made with chemical leavening instead of yeast. Chemical leavening is any substance that's added to the dough to create bubbles, which become trapped as the bread bakes and make a soft, open crumb. Usually, that means baking soda or baking powder. You could use baking soda in this recipe, which would react with the acids in the buttermilk and leaven the cornbread, but that neutralizes some of the flavor of those acids. I like to use baking powder, which preserves more of the tang of the buttermilk. For more about leavening, see page 19.

There are several styles of cornbread. Some are more cakelike, with lots of added sweetness and/or fat for tenderness. Some are more like solid polenta. I like my cornbread in the middle—the finer corn flour yields a really tender crumb. It's important to use good-quality, fresh cornmeal here—not some that has been sitting in the pantry for a year! Anson Mills is a great source for the cornmeal, and Bob's Red Mill makes corn flour. (Just make sure when you buy corn flour that you're not accidentally getting cornstarch, which is just the starchy endosperm of corn.)

You can also make corn flour yourself by grinding cornmeal in a spice grinder or mill and sifting it. If you can find it, it can be really fun to use an heirloom blue or red corn. If you like it a little sweeter, a drizzle of honey, maple syrup, or sorghum syrup can be added after baking.

Continued ～

Ingredients

2 tablespoons (28 grams) unsalted butter for the skillet, plus 4 tablespoons (57 grams)

1 cup (160 grams) corn flour

2 teaspoons (12 grams) baking powder

1 cup (140 grams) cornmeal

2 teaspoons (6 grams) kosher salt

1½ (366) cups buttermilk

2 medium eggs (120 grams), room temperature

Honey, maple syrup, or sorghum syrup, to drizzle (optional)

Preheat the oven to 400°F and place a rack in the middle position (get an adult assistant to help if needed). Warm an 8-inch cast-iron skillet in the oven with 2 tablespoons butter in it until the butter melts, then take it out of the oven and spread to coat the inside of the pan.

In a large mixing bowl, sift together the corn flour and the baking powder three times (this distributes the baking powder completely into the corn flour). Add the cornmeal and the salt and whisk to combine.

Warm the buttermilk on the stovetop to about 85°F (get an adult assistant to help if needed). Add the remaining 4 tablespoons butter and heat until the butter is just melted. Remove from the stovetop. Pour the warm buttermilk and butter into a medium bowl and add the eggs (make sure it's not so hot that the eggs get cooked). Whisk to combine.

Add the buttermilk mixture to the dry ingredients and stir with a wooden spoon until combined. Scrape the batter into the prepared skillet and use oven mitts to place it in the oven (get an adult assistant to help if needed). Set a timer for 20 minutes.

After 20 minutes, check to see if the cornbread is baking evenly. If the top is browning unevenly, use oven mitts to rotate the pan (get an adult assistant to help if needed).

Bake for 10 more minutes, then check to see if it's done by inserting a toothpick or cake tester into the middle (get an adult assistant to help if needed). It should come out mostly clean. If it comes out coated in wet batter, bake for 5 more minutes. Continue to check every 5 minutes until it's done.

Using oven mitts, remove the skillet from the oven and place it on a heatproof surface (such as the stovetop). Serve immediately, drizzled with honey, maple syrup, or sorghum syrup, if desired.

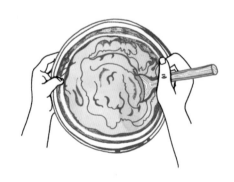

Sourdough Crackers

Makes 2 sheets of crackers, a little smaller than an 18 by 13-inch sheet pan

Difficulty level Beginner

Time from start of mixing to baked bread 1 hour

Baking vessel Two sheet pans

Mixer Optional

Ingredients

¾ cup (105 grams) whole wheat flour

¾ cup (105 grams) bread flour

2½ cups (215 grams) mature sourdough starter (see page 41)

⅓ cup (72 grams) extra-virgin olive oil, plus more to brush the dough

2 teaspoons (6 grams) kosher salt

Flaky sea salt for sprinkling on the dough

Herbs, grated cheese, sesame seeds, or poppy seeds, for topping

These crackers are a great way to use up leftover sourdough starter. The idea is to add just enough flour to your starter to stiffen it enough to roll out and toast to a delicate crispness. Since the starter is used for flavor more than leavening (you don't need the crackers to be light and fluffy), a starter at almost any stage will work for these crackers. You'll want to use starter that still smells appealing—you can even taste it to make sure it's still palatable. But since the flavor of the starter will be the flavor of the crackers, don't use something that's so far gone that it's unappealing or smells alcoholic.

Combine both flours, the sourdough starter, olive oil, and kosher salt in a medium bowl. Let rest for 20 minutes.

After 20 minutes, remove the dough from the bowl and place it on a lightly floured work surface. Knead the dough for 3 to 5 minutes, until it's smooth and strong. To knead it, flatten the dough a little on the surface. Fold the top half over the bottom and use the heel of your stronger hand to press the dough into itself. Rotate the dough one quarter-turn. Grab the top of the dough, fold it over again, and press into itself with the heel of your hand again. Continue rotating, folding, and pressing the dough until the kneading is complete.

Cover with a clean linen and let rest for 1 hour (you can also let it rest on the work surface). Preheat the oven to 400°F and place a rack in the middle position (get an adult assistant to help with baking if needed).

After 1 hour, the dough is ready to roll out. Divide it in half. Cut two sheets of parchment paper the size of a sheet pan.

Continued ∿

These are good for eating alone as a snack or for scooping or dipping anything from pimento cheese to spinach dip.

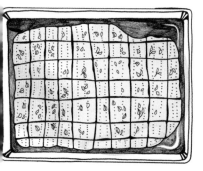

Use a rolling pin to roll the cracker dough out on a lightly-floured work surface until it's about ⅛ inch thick. Transfer the dough to a parchment-lined sheet pan and repeat with the second portion.

Lightly pierce the top of the dough with a fork about a dozen times. Brush the top of the dough lightly with olive oil and sprinkle with sea salt.

Using a pizza cutter or a paring knife, cut the cracker dough into 1-inch squares (or whatever size you'd like the crackers to be). Add any herbs, grated cheese, or other toppings of your choice at this point.

Use your oven mitts to place the crackers in the oven (get an adult assistant to help with baking if needed). Set a timer for 7 minutes, then using your oven mitts, rotate the pans. Bake for 5 more minutes, or until the crackers are light golden brown.

Use your oven mitts to remove the sheet pans from the oven and place them on a heatproof surface (such as the stovetop; get an adult assistant to help if needed).

Once the crackers are baked, they must cool all the way in order to be crisp. Remove them from the sheet pans (get an adult assistant to help if needed) and allow to cool on a cooling rack for at least an hour. If they cool and are still not crisp, you can re-toast them in a 350° oven for 5 to 7 minutes, until golden, then let cool again.

Store in an airtight container for up to 5 days.

Pretzels

Makes 6 large pretzels

Difficulty level Advanced (shaping, dipping in baking soda bath)

Time from start of mixing to baked bread 6 hours (plus 3 hours ahead to prepare the sponge)

Baking vessel Two sheet pans

Mixer Needed

A pretzel is a German style of bread that is shaped into a knot and has a salty, shiny crust—created by dipping the knotted dough into an alkaline bath. (Alkaline means having a pH greater than 7. An acid has a pH lower than 7, and 7 is neutral.) Lye is traditionally used to make this alkaline bath, but it is *so* alkaline that it is dangerous to use. We're going to use baking soda instead. Baking soda on its own will make a slightly alkaline solution with water, but we're going to bake it before we use it. That removes some of the moisture and makes it even a little more alkaline (but not nearly enough to be dangerous). You'll notice a slippery feeling when you dip the pretzels in the bath—that's the feeling of alkalinity. It's the same thing that makes a bar of soap (which is made with lye) feel slippery.

These pretzels are meant to be fluffy, soft, chewy, and salty. I like to eat them warm with a little smear of butter or mustard.

To make the sponge

In a medium mixing bowl, measure the warm water. Sprinkle the yeast on top of the water. Stir it with a spoon to dissolve the yeast. Add the flours to the bowl. Stir with a wooden spoon or your hand until the flour and water are combined well and there are no lumps. Cover the mixing bowl with a clean linen and let rest in warm spot on the countertop for 3 hours. It's ready to use when it has doubled in size and is very bubbly.

Continued ∿

Ingredients

Sponge (make 3 hours ahead)

½ cup (118 grams) warm water (about 85°F)

½ teaspoon (2 grams) instant dry yeast

⅓ cup (47 grams) bread flour

⅓ cup (47 grams) whole wheat flour

Dough

½ cup (118 grams) warm
water (about 85°F)

½ cup (120 grams) warm
whole milk (about 85°F)

2¼ cups (175 grams) sponge

½ teaspoon (2 grams)
instant dry yeast

1 tablespoon + 1 teaspoon
(12 grams) kosher salt

2½ cups (350 grams)
bread flour

⅓ cup (47 grams)
whole wheat flour

⅓ cup (43 grams)
whole rye flour

2 tablespoons (28 grams)
unsalted butter,
room temperature

Baking soda bath

½ cup (110 grams)
baking soda

2 cups (473 grams)
cool water

Flaky sea salt for sprinkling
on the shaped pretzels

To make the pretzel dough

In the bowl of a stand mixer fitted with a dough hook, place the warm water, warm milk, sponge, yeast, and kosher salt.

Measure the flours into a separate mixing bowl. Blend the butter into the flour by hand, a little bit at a time, until the pieces are about pea size (this is similar to what you do when making biscuits or pie crust).

Add the flour and butter mixture to the wet ingredients in the stand mixer bowl. Mix on low speed for 3 minutes, until all the ingredients are well mixed and a dough has started to form. Turn off the mixer and let the dough rest for 3 minutes.

After 3 minutes, mix on medium speed for 5 to 7 minutes, until a cohesive dough has formed. Take the dough out of the mixing bowl and place it in a clean bowl to proof. Cover the bowl with a clean linen and keep warm (around 80°F).

After 30 minutes, fold the dough. This will even out the temperature, re-distribute areas of more activity, and strengthen the gluten. To do so, loosen it from the edges of the bowl. Lift one side of the dough up, stretch it over the top, and press it back down into the bowl. Do this a few times until you have lifted, stretched, and folded all the dough.

Cover it again and let it rest for 30 minutes to 1 hour. After this last rest, it should have risen noticeably in the bowl. It doesn't need to double in size, but the change should be noticeable. You should be able to see bubbles in the dough. If you can see the rising and the bubbles, it's time to divide the dough. If not, let it rest for 15 more minutes. Check the dough every 10 to 15 minutes and divide it when you see a dramatic increase in size and lots of bubbles.

While the dough is rising, bake the baking soda for the bath. Preheat the oven to 250°F. Sprinkle the baking soda onto a baking pan (it's a little more than you need, but it will lose some weight and volume while you're baking it). Bake for 1 hour at 250°F. Remove the pan from the oven and let the baking soda cool before using.

Shaping

Step 1

Step 2

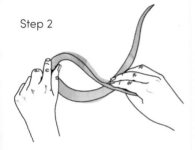

Step 3

Step 4

When the dough is ready to divide, lightly flour a worktable and turn the dough out onto it. Divide the dough into six equal-size pieces.

Pre-shape the pretzels (this prepares the gluten structures for the final shaping). Roll the pieces out into a thick log shape, about 4 inches long and 1 inch in diameter. Let the dough rest for 20 minutes.

While the dough is resting, prepare two sheet pans by lining them with silicone liners or parchment paper.

After 20 minutes, shape the pretzels. Roll one log out into a skinny snake shape about 18 inches long. To create the distinctive pretzel shape, pull the left end of your snake over toward the right side, about three-quarters of the way to the right end. Pick up the right end of the snake and fold it over the left, ending up in about the bottom of the loop you made when you folded the left side over. Pick up both of the ends and wrap them around each other once, to make a twist. You can manipulate the dough as much as you want here to get the desired shape. Once you have it just about where you want it, transfer it to the lined sheet pan. After you set it down on the sheet pan, you can rearrange it to look the way you want it.

Repeat with the remaining pieces of dough. Use a clean linen to loosely cover the shaped pretzels and place them in a warm, draft-free spot to rise for 1 hour.

After they have risen, place them in the freezer for 1 hour.

While they are freezing, prepare the baking soda bath. To do so, mix the baked baking soda and cool water well in a glass bowl or a ceramic bowl or baking dish that is big enough to dip a pretzel in (don't use metal, as this can react with the baking soda and cause a funny taste).

Preheat the oven to 400°F and place racks in the top and bottom thirds of the oven (ask an adult assistant for help if needed).

Continued ∿

Once they are frozen, put them in the baking soda bath one at a time. Let them sit in the bath for about 3 minutes each. Place them back on the lined sheet pans again. (You may need to re-shape them a little.) Sprinkle them with flaky sea salt while they are still wet.

Once all of the pretzels are dipped and salted, you can bake them (they don't need to thaw). Using oven mitts, place the pans carefully in the oven, one on each rack (ask an adult assistant for help if needed). Set a timer for 10 minutes.

After 10 minutes, take a peek at them. If they are baking unevenly, use your oven mitts to rotate the sheet pans back to front and top to bottom.

Bake for 7 to 10 minutes longer, until the pretzels are golden brown all over. Using your oven mitts, carefully remove the trays from the oven (get an adult assistant to help if needed). Let them cool on the stovetop for about 5 minutes, then use a spatula to transfer them from the sheet pans to cooling racks.

These are best when eaten warm! To keep, store them in a sealed container for up to 3 days. They can be re-warmed to serve.

Grissini

Makes About 24 bread-
    sticks

Difficulty level Beginner

**Time from start of mixing
to baked bread** 4 hours
(plus 3 hours ahead to
prepare the sponge)

Baking vessel Sheet pan

Mixer Needed

Ingredients

Sponge
(make 3 hours ahead)

½ cup (118 grams) warm
    water (about 85°F)

½ teaspoon (2 grams)
    instant dry yeast

1 cup (140 grams)
    whole wheat flour

Dough

⅔ cup (157 grams) warm
    water (about 85°F)

1 tablespoon (21 grams)
    honey

Continued ⌇

Grissini are a classic Italian snack that's kind of a hybrid between a cracker and a breadstick. If you like making playdough snakes, you'll love making grissini.

Grissini is a very old type of bread in Italy, and legend has it that they were created as an easily digestible bread for a young duke who was a sickly child. After several years of eating grissini, the young duke faced the French in a big battle and won, resulting in him being crowned King of Sicily.

To make the sponge

In a small mixing bowl, measure the warm water. Sprinkle the yeast on top and stir with a spoon to dissolve the yeast. Add the flour to the bowl. Stir with a wooden spoon or your hand until the flour and water are combined well and there are no lumps. Cover the mixing bowl with a clean linen and let the dough rest in a warm spot on the countertop for about 3 hours. It's ready to use when it has doubled in size and is very bubbly.

To make the dough

Remove the bowl of a stand mixer and measure the water, honey, olive oil, and salt into it. Sprinkle the yeast over the water mixture and stir to dissolve. Stir the sponge (just to break it up a little) into the rest of the wet ingredients.

Continued ⌇

1 tablespoon (14 grams) extra-virgin olive oil, plus more for brushing

2 teaspoons (6 grams) kosher salt

½ teaspoon (2 grams) instant dry yeast

2⅔ cups (215 grams) sponge

1½ cups (210 grams) all-purpose flour

Sesame seeds, nigella seeds, chopped rosemary, or chopped thyme, for topping (optional)

Measure the flour into the wet ingredients and return the bowl to the mixer, fitted with the dough hook attachment. Mix on low speed for 3 minutes, until the ingredients are combined well. Scrape the sides and bottom of the bowl well to make sure everything is completely incorporated. Let rest for 3 minutes.

Mix on medium speed (or knead on a clean, lightly-floured work surface) for 3 to 5 minutes, until the dough is strong and supple. If the dough seems like it's starting to tear, let it rest for a minute before resuming mixing.

Once the dough is mixed, transfer it to a clean mixing bowl. Cover the bowl with a clean linen and place it in warm, draft-free spot. Let it rise for 1 hour. (Alternatively, you can put the dough in the refrigerator overnight and continue the steps on the next day.)

Once the dough has risen a little bit, you're ready to divide the dough. Scoop it out of the bowl (a bowl scraper is handy for this, but you can also use a spatula or just your fingers) onto a clean work surface. Pat the dough out into a large, thin rectangle, about 8 by 12 inches and ½-inch thick, with the 8-inch side facing you. Use your metal dough scraper or a knife to cut a ½-inch piece of dough off the side of the rectangle closest to you. Roll it out on the table so that it is about 10 inches long and very skinny. It's okay of it's not perfectly uniform; these are supposed to be rustic.

As you shape each one, place it on a sheet pan lined with parchment paper about ½ inch away from its neighbor. Continue until all the pieces of dough are shaped.

Brush them very lightly them with extra-virgin olive oil. If you want to sprinkle any seeds or seasonings on, now's the time.

Allow them to rest for 15 minutes. Preheat the oven to 350°F and place a rack in the middle position (get an adult assistant to help if needed).

After 15 minutes, use your oven mitts to place the sheet pan very carefully in the oven (get an adult assistant to help if needed). Set a timer for 10 minutes, then check to see how they are baking. If necessary, use oven mitts to rotate the pan so that they bake evenly. Bake for 7 to 10 more minutes, then check to see if they're done. They should be a light golden brown. Note: Make sure to keep a very close eye on them in the oven—these can burn very quickly because each uses such a small amount of dough.

When they're done baking, use oven mitts to remove the pan carefully from the oven (get an adult assistant to help if needed) and place it on a heatproof surface (such as the stovetop).

Let cool for about 10 minutes, then transfer to a cooling rack. Let cool for at least 30 minutes (they must cool all the way to be crispy.) If they still aren't crispy after they cool, you can re-toast them in a 350°F oven for 5 to 7 minutes until golden, then let cool again. You can keep them in a sealed container or a bag on the countertop for up to 4 days.

These are good for a snack or an appetizer— I love to put a vase of them on the table before a dinner party —they make a stunning edible centerpiece.

This bread is good just-baked with some butter or cheese. I also love a simple sandwich on a baguette with only a few ingredients, like cheese and tomatoes. Baguettes lend themselves very well to sweet toppings, like jam. They're also a showstopping picnic star.

Baguettes

Makes 2 baguettes

Difficulty level
Intermediate (shaping)

Time from start of mixing to baked bread 6 hours (plus 3 hours ahead to prepare the sponge)

Baking vessel Baking stone or steel

Mixer Needed

Ingredients

Sponge
(make 3 hours ahead)

⅔ cup (157 grams) cool water (about 70°F)

¼ teaspoon (1 gram) instant dry yeast

1 cup (140 grams) bread flour

A classic baguette is one of the more fun breads to make. There's something so dramatic about the long shape and the distinctive score. Few other breads beg to be eaten immediately with very little alongside it, maybe just a touch of cultured butter and cheese. At Tartine, bakers have worked on baguettes for years, tweaking them and improving them in a never-ending quest for the perfect baguette. They still haven't stopped, and the ritual of gathering around a fresh baguette to cut it open to investigate the crumb, taste it, and decide how to make it better the next day will always be one of my favorite memories as a baker at Tartine.

To make the sponge

In a small mixing bowl, measure the cool water. Sprinkle the yeast on the water and stir with a spoon to dissolve it. Add the flour to the bowl. Stir with a wooden spoon or your hand until the flour and water are combined well and there are no lumps. Cover the mixing bowl with a clean linen and let rest in a warm spot on the countertop for 3 hours. It's ready to use when it has doubled in size and is very bubbly.

Continued ⌁

Dough

1 cup (236 grams) warm
water (about 80°F)

1 teaspoon (4 grams) instant
dry yeast

3⅓ cups (287 grams)
sponge

2 cups (280 grams)
bread flour

1 tablespoon (9 grams)
kosher salt

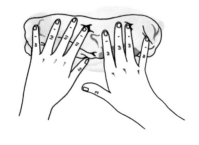

To make the dough

Remove the bowl of a stand mixer from the body of the mixer. Measure the warm water into it. Sprinkle the yeast over the water and stir to dissolve. Stir the sponge into the water and yeast mixture.

Measure the flour into the water and yeast mixture and return the bowl to the mixer, fitted with the dough hook attachment. Mix on low speed for 3 minutes, until all the ingredients are combined well. Scrape the sides of the bowl and let the dough rest for 20 minutes.

After 20 minutes, measure the salt into the bowl, then mix on medium speed for about 7 minutes, until the dough is strong and supple. If the dough seems like it's starting to tear, let it rest for 2 minutes before resuming mixing.

Transfer the dough to a clean mixing bowl. Cover the bowl with a clean linen and place it in warm spot. Let it rise for 45 minutes.

After 45 minutes, fold the dough. This will even out the temperature, re-distribute areas of more activity, and strengthen the gluten. To do so, loosen it from the edges of the bowl. Lift the side of the dough up, stretch it over the top, and press it back down into the bowl. Do this a few times until you have lifted, stretched, and folded all the dough. Cover it again and let it rise for 45 more minutes.

After 45 minutes, it should have risen noticeably in the bowl. You should be able to see bubbles in the dough. If you can see the rising and the bubbles, it's time to divide the dough. If not, let it rest for 15 more minutes. Check the dough every 10 to 15 minutes and divide it when you see an increase in size and bubbles.

To divide the dough, scoop it out of the bowl (a bowl scraper is handy for this, but you can also use a spatula or just your fingers) onto a work surface. Divide the dough equally in half (each half should weigh about 400 grams).

To shape the loaves, pat each portion of dough gently into a rectangle, roughly 12 by 4 inches. A long side of the rectangle should be closest to you. Shape one loaf at a time. Using your fingertips, roll the top edge toward you, almost as if you're rolling up a carpet. Press the rolled part gently into the flat part as you continue to roll toward you. Once it's all rolled up, press the seam where the bottom edge meets the rolled-up part of the loaf together. Roll the dough back and forth under your hands to taper the ends. Repeat for the other portion of dough. Lightly flour your work surface if it sticks.

Place the shaped loaves on a clean, well-floured linen laid over a sheet pan. Use the ends of the floured linen or another piece of clean floured linen to cover the baguettes and let them rise on the countertop for 1 hour. After an hour, they should have risen noticeably. If you poke the loaves gently with your fingertips, they should feel full of air and spring back slowly. Once they have risen noticeably, then place them in the fridge to chill for 1 hour.

An hour before you are ready to bake (or according to the manufacturer's instructions on your baking surface), preheat a baking stone or steel set in the middle of the oven to 400°F (get an adult assistant to help if needed).

Once the baguettes are ready to bake, gently tip them onto your baguette (or pizza) peel, then roll them off the peel and onto the baking surface in the oven (get an adult assistant to help if needed). Try to keep the seam side down. Use a razor or a very sharp knife to draw a few quick lines lengthwise down the top of the baguette.

Most baking surfaces will have room to bake both baguettes at once, but if you are baking them one at a time, keep the other baguette in the fridge until you're ready to bake it.

Bake for 15 to 20 minutes. The loaves are finished when they are an even medium brown all over the top. If they look speckled or blonde, give them a few more minutes.

When done baking, use oven mitts and a spatula or a peel to remove the baguettes from the oven (get an adult assistant to help if needed.) Set them on a cooling rack and let cool for at least 30 minutes.

You can keep the baguettes in a bread box or bag on the countertop for up to 4 days.

Sourdough Bread

Makes Three 8½ by 4½-inch loaves or two 8-inch boules

Difficulty level Advanced (fermentation, shaping, baking)

Time from start of mixing to baked bread 7 hours (leaven prepared 3 hours before)

Baking vessel Three 8½ by 4½-inch bread pans or two 8- or 9-inch boule baskets

Mixer Needed

Making sourdough bread is a never-ending journey of learning. Every day has its own set of conditions, every batch of flour is slightly different. I could spend the rest of my life making sourdough bread and never arrive at a place where I've perfected it every time and have no more to learn.

This bread can be made in a pan or in a basket. I recommend mastering the recipe in pan form first, since a pan is a lot more forgiving (it holds its shape even if the dough is wet or the shaping isn't perfect). Instructions for making boules are included at the end for more advanced bakers.

I always refer to "starter" as the culture of flour, water, yeast, and bacteria that I feed to keep it going, and to "leaven" as the culture I prepare in order to raise the bread. So you'll read both "feed the starter regularly for a few days" and "feed the leaven first thing in the morning, about 3 hours before you plan to mix your dough." There is a lot of variation in terms among bakers, but this usage is pretty common.

In order to start your own starter, follow the instructions on page 41. It's a good idea to give a starter about 2 weeks to get established before using it for bread. Alternatively, you can get a pinch of starter from someone who already has one established.

The amount of dough here is a little more than for the other recipes in this book. That's because I want you to have enough to make two 1-kilogram boules (a standard size for most bread-proofing baskets). If you make pan loaves, you'll have enough for three pans, or you could make two pans and use the remainder of the dough for a sheet-pan pizza by spreading it out thin and putting some toppings on before baking in a preheated 400° oven.

Continued ∿

This bread is good for
an excellent all-around bread—
good for toast, sandwiches, or
simply eating fresh with butter.

Sourdough Bread
Continued 〰

Ingredients

Leaven
(make 3 hours ahead)

½ cup (118 grams) warm
water (about 85°F)

½ cup (70 grams)
bread flour

½ cup (70 grams)
whole wheat flour

⅓ cup (45 grams) mature
sourdough starter
formula (page 41)

Dough

3¼ cups (767 grams) warm
water (about 85°F)

3⅔ cups (300 grams)
mature leaven

5¾ cups (805 grams)
bread flour

1½ cups (210 grams)
whole wheat flour

2 tablespoons + 1 teaspoon
(41 grams) kosher salt

Extra-virgin olive oil, for
the pans and brushing
the loaves, or flour
for the baskets

To make the leaven

The morning of the day you want to mix your dough, use a mature starter to feed your leaven. In a wide-mouth quart-size mason jar, measure the warm water, the flours, and the mature starter. Mix well with your hand to combine. Leave it in a warm, draft-free spot until it has risen significantly and shows lot of bubbles. (If you like, you can tie a string or rubber band around the jar at the place where the top of the starter is right after you mix it—this makes it easier to keep track of how much it grows.)

It will usually take 3 hours or so to mature, but it may take a little longer if the environment is cool. Make sure to wait until the leaven has risen and is bubbly before using. You can also smell it to see if it's ready. Unripe leaven smells like fresh flour or pancake batter. Ripe leaven smells a little sour, a little floral, a little creamy—almost like yogurt. It's a good idea to smell it often and get used to how it smells at different stages.

To make the dough

In a large mixing bowl (preferably glass so you can see your dough as it develops), measure the warm water, mature leaven, bread flour, and whole wheat flour. Mix well with your hand until all the ingredients are combined, about 3 minutes. Use your plastic scraper to remove the dough that is stuck to your hand and scrape it back into the bowl.

Cover the bowl with a clean linen and let rest in a warm, draft-free spot for 30 minutes.

After 30 minutes, measure the salt into the dough. Dampen your stronger hand and squeeze the salt into the dough for a minute; don't worry if it comes apart a bit—it will come back together in the next steps.

Mixing

1. Combine wet and dry ingredients

2. Squeeze and pinch until dough comes together

3. Stretch and fold well to develop a strong, elastic dough

Fold the dough. Loosen the edges of the dough from the bowl, using your damp hand and a damp plastic dough scraper. Set the scraper down and lift up the edge of the dough farthest from you, grabbing a healthy pinch and stretching it upward. Fold that handful over the top of the bowl of dough and press it down into the dough. Take up another healthy handful from right next to where you grabbed the last one. Stretch, fold, and press it down.

Continue this stretching and folding, going around the dough a few times until it has all been stretched and folded and feels strong and cohesive. If the dough is too stiff to stretch and fold, you can splash in a tiny extra bit of water.

Once you have a strong, cohesive dough, scrape your hands and the edges of the bowl with a plastic bowl scraper. Cover the bowl with a clean linen and let rest for 30 minutes in a warm, draft-free spot.

After 30 minutes, fold the dough to build a little more gluten strength. Dampen your hand and use the same lifting and stretching action you did during the mixing phase, but go around the bowl only once, folding about five times. Cover the bowl again and let it rest in a warm, draft-free spot for 30 minutes.

After 30 minutes, do the same thing as last time: dampen your hands and lift, stretch, and fold the dough, going around the bowl until all the dough has been stretched and folded. Cover the bowl again and let rest for 1 hour in a warm draft-free spot.

After an hour, the dough should have risen noticeably in the bowl. There should be some evidence of air bubbles on the top of the dough, and if you pull the dough away from the sides of the bowl, you can see more bubbles. If this has happened, it is ready to divide and pre-shape. If not, keep it covered and warm and check every 15 minutes until you can see bubbles and rising.

Continued ∿

To divide and pre-shape the dough, dampen your hands and scoop the dough out onto your work surface. Divide it in half, then gently shape each half into a round ball. Let the balls rest on your work surface for 30 minutes.

While the dough balls are resting, prepare two 8½ by 4½-inch bread pans. Using a pastry brush or your fingers, coat the inside of the pans with olive oil and set aside.

After 30 minutes, *very* lightly flour the tops of each ball and your work surface. Use your bench knife or plastic scraper to loosen the ball from the table. Flip it over so that the floured side of the dough is lying on the floured work surface. The part facing you now should be free of flour.

Pat the dough gently into a rectangle about 12 inches by 6 inches. The shorter sides of the rectangle should be at the top and bottom, and the longer sides should be on the right- and left-hand sides. Using your fingertips, roll the top edge toward you, almost as if you're rolling up a carpet. Press the rolled part gently into the flat part as you continue to roll toward yourself. Once it's all rolled up, press the seam where the bottom edge meets the rolled-up part of the loaf together. Place the shaped loaf into the oiled pan with the seam on the bottom. Repeat for the second loaf.

If you'd like to delay baking until the next day, you can put the loaves in the refrigerator overnight at this point.

Let the loaves rise for an hour, covered, or up to two until they have risen taller than the loaf pans. If you poke the loaves gently with your fingertip, they should feel full of air and spring back slowly.

While the loaves are rising for the final time, preheat the oven to 450°F and place a rack in the middle position (get an adult assistant to help if needed).

Once the loaves have risen in the pan, use a clean pastry brush to brush the top of the loaves with olive oil so they are evenly coated. Then score the loaves (for more about scoring, see page 159). Use sharp kitchen scissors to snip the top of each loaf six to eight times at even distances apart (get an adult assistant to help if needed).

You can also bake this bread in a cloche or a Dutch oven. The closed chamber traps the steam as the loaf bakes. This allows the loaf to rise and form a beautiful, shiny crust. Preheat the Dutch oven in the preheating oven. Place the loaf on a piece of parchment paper and score. Remove the heated Dutch oven from the oven with oven mitts, then use the parchment to carefully place the scored loaf into the hot Dutch oven and place the lid on top. Place the Dutch oven back in the oven and bake for 20 minutes. After 20 minutes, remove the hot lid and bake for another 10 to 15 minutes, until the top is golden brown. Carefully remove the loaf from the Dutch oven and let cool on a rack.

Using oven mitts, place the pans gently on the rack in the middle of the oven (get an adult assistant to help if needed). Close the oven door and set a timer for 20 minutes.

After 20 minutes, take a peek at your bread. If it looks like it is darker on one part of the loaves, use oven mitts to turn the pans half a turn so that they will finish baking evenly (get an adult assistant to help if needed).

Bake for 10 to 15 more minutes. The loaves are finished baking when they are an even medium brown all over the top. If they look speckled or blonde, give them a few more minutes.

When they're done baking, use oven mitts to remove the pans from the oven (get an adult assistant to help if needed) and set them on a heatproof surface (such as a stovetop) to cool for 10 minutes.

After 10 minutes, gently remove the loaves from the pans (get an adult assistant to help if needed). Set the loaves on a cooling rack and let cool for at least 1 hour.

This bread keeps well. It can be eaten fresh for a few days. If it starts to seem stale, cut and toast slices or warm the whole loaf in a very hot oven.

Variations

This bread is a great blank canvas. Add any ingredients you want during the first mixing phase, such as your favorite toasted seeds, like sesame. Or try adding some golden raisins and pumpkin seeds. Other favorite additions are roasted garlic and chopped rosemary. Sprinkle some seeds on top, too, after you've brushed the loaves with olive oil.

Continued ⁓

To shape into boules

Proceed as above, up to the stage where you're ready to shape (the pre-shape is the same.)

Prepare two round bread baskets, each roughly 8 or 9 inches in diameter. Line them with clean linen and flour the linen well.

Very **lightly flour your work surface and the tops of your dough balls.** Working with one at a time, use your bench knife or plastic scraper to loosen the ball from the table. Flip it over so that the floured side of the dough is lying on the floured work surface. The part facing you now should be free of flour.

Gently pat the dough just a little bit, into a circle, roughly 9 inches in diameter. Pinch a piece of the dough farthest from you and very gently stretch it up and toward you, pinning it to the center of your circle. You can hold it here with your other hand if you need to. Now pinch another section of the dough to the side of the one you just folded over and do the same: stretch it, fold it over, and pin it down. Proceed this way around the whole loaf, about five times, until the whole thing has been gathered into a ball.

Hold the ball in your hand and pinch the gathered parts together a little if needed to make them stick. Set the dough down on a section of the work surface with NO flour, the pinched side down. Cup your hands around the dough and gently round it a little more, pulling the ball toward you a little bit, then turning it and pulling it toward you again, until the dough ball is evenly rounded.

Use your bench knife to lift the dough ball from the table and place it seam side UP in your lined and floured basket. Repeat with the other ball.

If you'd like to bake the next day, you can put the loaves, covered, into the refrigerator overnight at this point.

Let the loaves rest for an hour, or up to two, until they rise a bit in the baskets. If you poke the loaves gently with your fingertip, they should feel full of air and spring back slowly.

While the loaves are rising the final time, preheat a baking stone or steel on a rack in the middle of a 450°F oven for 30 minutes to 1 hour, according to the manufacturer's instructions and the type of oven you have (ask an adult assistant for help if needed). If possible, use an internal oven thermometer or a laser thermometer to track the temperature of the oven. Fill a spray bottle with clean cool water and keep it handy.

To bake the loaves, lightly flour the exposed dough. The part that is facing you, currently the top, will be the bottom when you're baking the loaf—you want to lightly flour it so that it doesn't stick to your baking surface. If you like, you can blend a little semolina or rice flour into the flour you use to dust the bottoms—that will really keep it from sticking.

Open the oven carefully and, using oven mitts, pull the rack out enough for you to be able to tip both loaves easily onto the baking surface (ask an adult assistant for help if needed). Tip the loaves out of each basket onto your baking stone or steel. Use a pair of sharp kitchen scissors to quickly snip the top of both loaves six to eight times. Alternatively, use a sharp knife to make small slits or slashes in the top of the loaf.

Gently spray some water into the oven—enough to get a noticeable amount of steam (a little can land on the loaves, but don't spray them directly). Close the oven and set a timer for 20 minutes.

After 20 minutes, check to see if the loaves are baking evenly. Using oven mitts, rotate them if necessary (ask an adult assistant for help if needed). Bake for 15 more minutes and then check to see if the loaves are done. They should be medium-dark brown all over.

Remove the boules from the oven using oven mitts and a sturdy spatula or peel (get an adult assistant to help you if needed). Place them on a cooling rack and cool for 1 hour.

The serving and storage instructions are the same as for pan loaves.

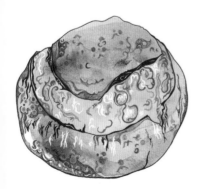

Intro to Baker's Math

You don't need to read or master this section to bake beautiful bread. This is pretty advanced stuff, but it's a really important part of becoming an expert baker. Unlocking baker's math is a bit like unlocking a secret language that will suddenly let you see behind the curtain of a bread recipe. Once you understand this stuff, you will have a very good idea of what a recipe, or formula in bread bakers' language, will make before you even try it. You'll also be able to wield this secret language to make anything you can dream up.

I've chosen to include this here because even though it seems daunting to many adults, I absolutely think kids can grasp it and benefit from it. I believe in you.

Baker's math is a system of math that is used just for bread. In it, all the ingredients are expressed as a percentage of the total flour weight. **The flour weight is always 100%.** If the water is 75%, that's 75% of whatever the total flour weight is. If your salt is 2%, that's 2% of the total flour weight. It's easiest to see this when looking at a simple formula, expressed in grams.

Say you are making a recipe that calls for 100 grams of flour (it's a teensy tiny loaf). That means your total flour is 100 grams. Your water is 75%, so that's 75 grams. Your sourdough starter is 25%, so that's 25 grams. Your salt is 2%, so that's 2 grams.

If you have the percentages written out, in order to find out what the amount of an ingredient is, you calculate that percentage *of* the total flour weight (remember, "of" means "multiply" in math language). So if your formula says your water is 75%, you multiply 75% (or 0.75, since a percentage is an expression of a part of 100) times the total flour weight.

In this formula, that would be 0.75 x 100 grams = 75 grams.

Said another way, 75% of 100 grams is 75 grams.

When you write the whole formula out, it looks like this:

100 grams flour (100%)

75 grams water (75%)

25 grams sourdough starter (25%)

2 grams salt (2%)

Now, say you want to make the same formula with 1,000 grams (or 1 kilogram) of flour instead. Your flour weight is still 100%, in this case 1,000 grams. So all of the percentages are calculated against 1,000 grams.

To find the water, you calculate 75% of 1,000, or 0.75 x 1000 = 750 grams.

To find the sourdough starter, you calculate 25% of 1000, or 0.25 x 1000 = 250 grams, and so on.

Knowing the percentages allows to you understand how all of the ingredients interact with each other. It's very useful to know the hydration percentage (the percentage of wet ingredients relative to the flour) of a dough before you make it—that will allow you to guess whether it's going to be a soft, sticky dough or a stiff, dry one. You can make some decisions about what you can expect and how to handle the dough if you have that information. Eventually, you can experiment with formulas by changing the hydration percentage a little and even come up with your own.

The next phase of baker's math is coming up with the whole thing from scratch. Say I want to make a pizza dough recipe. I know I want it to be a little stiffer and easier to handle, so I want the hydration (amount of water relative to flour) to be a little lower at 65%. Other than that, for this dough, I'm going to keep the formula the same as the above dough.

- 100% flour
- 65% water
- 25% sourdough starter
- 2% salt

But how do I know what the flour amount is so I can calculate the rest of the amounts? This is the really cool part. If you figure out two other numbers, the total dough and the total percentage, you can calculate the total flour amount.

The total dough is determined by how much you want to make. Let's say we want to make five pizza dough balls, each weighing 200 grams. That's 200 grams x 5, or 1,000 grams. So our total dough is 1,000 grams. (If we only wanted to make four dough balls, our total dough would be 200 grams x 4, or 800 grams.)

The total percentage is just the number you get from adding all the percentages together: 100% + 65% + 25% + 2% = 192%.

Now, if you divide that total dough by the total percentage, you get the total flour. The formula looks like this:

Total dough divided by total percentage = total flour or, in our case, 1,000.00 divided by 1.92% = 521 grams of flour

So the total amount of flour is 521 grams. Now you can calculate the rest of the percentages against that one. For the water, 65% of 521 is 339 (0.65 x 521 = 339). For the

Total Flour Formula

$$\frac{\text{total dough}}{\text{total percentage}} = \text{total flour}$$

sourdough starter, 25% of 521 is 130 (0.25 x 520 = 130). For the salt, 2% of 520 is 10 (0.02 x 521 = 10)

The formula looks like this:

100% flour = 521 grams

65% water = 339 grams

25% sourdough starter = 130 grams

2% salt = 10 grams

Total percentage = 192%

Total dough = 1,000 grams

Total flour = 521 grams

You can add up all the ingredients to see if you got the final dough amount you were expecting (the total weight of all the ingredients should equal the total dough).

521 + 339 + 130 + 10 = 1,000 grams

You did it! You'll have exactly five pizza dough balls weighing 200 grams each. You're a mega bread wizard.

Formulas

New Sourdough Starter p.41

water	80%
bread flour	50%
whole wheat flour	50%

Honey Whole Wheat Bread
p.49

Sponge

water	80%
yeast	1%
bread flour	50%
whole wheat flour	50%

Dough

water	80%
yeast	1%
sponge	100%
honey	8%
whole wheat flour	50%
bread flour	50%
kosher salt	2.5%

Challah p.72

water	43%
yeast	.75%
sunflower seed oil	12%
large eggs, room temperature	25%
granulated sugar	11%
kosher salt	1.5%
all-purpose flour	100%

Baguettes p.141

Sponge

water	75%
yeast	0.5%
bread flour	100%

Dough

water	75%
yeast	0.5%
sponge	100%
bread flour	100%
kosher salt	3%

Sourdough Bread p.144

Starter

warm water	100%
bread flour	50%
whole wheat flour	50%
mature sourdough starter	25%

Dough

warm water	75%
bread flour	80%
whole wheat flour	20%
leaven	20%
kosher salt	2.5%

Key Terms

Bulk fermentation (see also Rising on page 159; Bulk fermentation on page 26 in Steps of Bread Making). This is the stage of dough fermentation after the end of mixing and before dividing for pre-shaping or shaping. During this stage, the dough gains volume from the gaseous byproducts of yeast and bacterial fermentation, develops strength and gluten, and increases in acidity and flavor. Bulk fermentation can take 1½ hours for a warm dough with lots of added yeast or up to 48 hours for a sourdough with naturally occurring yeast kept in the refrigerator. Theoretically you could go even longer than that, although the gluten eventually begins to break down over time.

Crumb/open crumb. The crumb is the interior part of the bread, as opposed to the crust. The crumb is characterized by a soft, squishy web of gluten, punctuated by bubbles created through fermentation. The bubbles can be large or small, depending on what type of flour you use, how wet your dough is, how you mixed it, how it was fermented, and what other ingredients besides flour and water are in your dough— among other factors. When the fermentation bubbles are large and irregular, we say the bread has an "open crumb."

Development. When used in the context of bread baking, it means gluten development or dough development. It is a loose term that covers a lot of complex changes, including gluten formation and relaxation and yeast and bacterial fermentation and the resulting changes to the dough, such as aeration.

Gluten. Gluten is the protein responsible for the strong, stretchy character of wheat dough. Gluten, found in wheat, barley, rye, and triticale, is actually a protein made up of two simpler proteins, glutenin and gliadin. When water is added to flour and given some agitation and some time, glutenin and gliadin link together and form chains. The longer and stronger these chains form, the more "development" we say a dough has. A dough can also become overdeveloped and start to break down. One of the skills of a bread baker is being able to feel this development and know when enough development has been achieved to move onto the next step. For more, see Baking Science on page 19.

Fermentation. This is the process by which a substance breaks down into simpler substances. In reference to bread, this means that complex carbohydrates are broken down by yeast and bacteria into simpler sugars, then into carbon dioxide gas, ethanol, and lactic acid. The carbon dioxide gas becomes trapped in the dough, causing the bubbles that make a crumb open, and the ethanol and lactic acid create flavor and improve the texture of the dough. This is a *very* simple explanation of what is a pretty complex process, but those are the basics. For more, see page 19.

Formula/baker's math. Bakers usually refer to "formulas" instead of "recipes" for what goes into the dough. This is because bread formulas are based on baker's math, a system by which all the ingredients in the dough are measured against the total flour weight. This makes it easy to scale a recipe up or down (make more or less dough). It also makes it easy to make adjustments to doughs, like increasing or decreasing hydration. It creates a common language for bakers to use when talking about how they make their bread. Once a baker has learned baker's math, he or she can make a very educated guess about what a bread will be like just by looking at the formula. (For more, see Intro to Baker's Math on page 153.) I have used the word *recipes* for most of the book, just to keep it easy, but where I'm specifically talking about baker's math or percentages, I've used *formulas* for accuracy.

Hydration. Roughly, this is the amount of wet ingredients relative to the dry ingredients in a dough. This term is most often used to refer to simple country-style doughs or ones like pizza dough, with just flour, water, salt, and maybe a very few other ingredients. The hydration in a formula using baker's math refers to the percentage of water relative to the total flour weight. So if a dough is 80 percent hydration, that means that the water is 80 percent of the flour by weight (80 percent of 1,000, or 80 percent x 1,000 = 800). A dough with 1 kilo (or 1,000 grams) of flour that has 800 grams of water is 80 percent hydration.

Higher hydration doughs tend to be stretchier, stickier, and harder to work with, although they can also be more tender, more open, and last longer once baked into bread. Lower hydration doughs are stiffer and sturdier, but they will make a bread with a tighter and sturdier crumb. This is a very general rule, though, especially since flour varies so much. A low-protein flour (like pastry flour) dough at 70 percent hydration might be softer and stretchier than a high-protein flour (like bread flour) dough at 80 percent hydration. This seems complicated, but the more you bake and the more you pay attention to formulas and flours, the more it will all start to make sense.

Incorporation. The inclusion of an ingredient into a dough. An example is the incorporation of sesame seeds into sourdough to make sesame sourdough.

Pre-ferment. Any portion of dough that is fermented before being incorporated into the final dough. Sourdough starter and sponge are both pre-ferments. There are lots of different names for pre-ferments: leaven, levain, and mother are some terms that refer to pre-ferments made with a portion of naturally fermented flour; poolish, biga, and sponge refer to pre-ferments that are made by mixing flour and water (and sometimes a very few other ingredients) with commercial yeast. In this book, we use the term *sponge* to refer to the pre-ferments in most of the recipes. For more, see page 36.

Pre-mix. The very first phase of mixing, just to hydrate the flour.

Proofing. The final stage of allowing the dough to rise after shaping. For more, see page 27.

Rest and relax. Gluten gets strong and tight as you mix the dough. It is often beneficial to allow the dough to relax for a few moments in between mixing and kneading.

Rising (see also Bulk fermentation on page 157). This refers to the period after the end of mixing and before dividing and/or shaping, during which the yeast and bacteria start to ferment and generate gas, which causes the dough to rise.

Scoring. Slashing, docking, or snipping the top of a fully proofed loaf before baking, to allow gasses trapped under the top of the loaf to escape and to allow the loaf to rise to its full potential in the oven.

Sponge. A pre-ferment made with commercial yeast (see also Pre-ferment on page 36).

Folding the dough. Most bread recipes have you "punch down" or de-gas the dough at some point during the rising phase. I prefer a gentler "fold" to a "punch down." It is important to get new oxygen into the fermenting dough and to redistribute any areas of greater yeast activity to areas with more flour for the yeast to consume. Folding the dough can also make sure that your dough is an even temperature throughout. To fold a dough, loosen it from the sides of the bowl. Stretch the dough up from underneath and fold it over the top a few times.

Yeast. A microscopic organism in the fungi kingdom responsible for much of the flavor and character of bread. Yeast consumes the starches in hydrated flour and excretes gases and acids that give bread its flavor and texture (see What Is Yeast? on page 38).

Acknowledgments

I never realized how much of a village it takes to make a book until I tried to make one.

Thank you, from the bottom of my heart, to:

Lorena Jones, for believing in me and taking a chance on me.

Kitty Cowles, for seeing me as I've always wanted to be seen.

Alanna Hale, for being my biggest cheering section, process coach, style inspo, bread buddy, and best girl. Oh yeah and for making these absolutely gorgeous photos.

Chad Robertson, for too many things to count over so many years, above all for your friendship. And that board.

Claire Mack, for going so far above and beyond with your space, props, and mad style even while your actual basement was flooding. Your generosity of spirit is staggering.

Hannah Wear and Marie Bose, who took all of my sketchy recipe notes and turned them into beautiful bread.

Hennie Haworth, for picking this project up and running with it.

Emma Rudolph and Kim Keller, for doing so much heavy lifting to make it all make sense.

Isabelle Gioffredi, for listening to all my quirky feedback and taking it so gracefully and making this book so beautiful, and to you and Emma Campion for seeing and translating my vision.

To all the friends and bakers and baker friends who cheered me on from the sidelines: Mahasti Vafie, Matt Jones, Samin Nosrat, and my beloved Tartine crew—Veronica Cates, Meg Fisher, Lisa Chun, and so many more. You all inspire me.

To Trac and Aine, for being our pod and chosen family and for giving me time, space, food, and love during some crazy times.

To Aria Ashton, my seventh-grade poetry buddy and passion fruit cake soup accomplice.

To Mom and Dad, for setting me on this path and being absolute next level grandparents.

To Ben and June, for being aces recipe testers and inspiring this book.

To Jay, for absolutely everything, always.

Index

Library of Congress Control Number: 2022936115

Paperback ISBN: 978-1-9848-6046-0
eBook ISBN: 978-1-9848-6047-7

Printed in China

Acquiring editor: Lorena Jones | Project editor:
  Emma Rudolph | Production editor: Kim Keller
Designer: Isabelle Gioffredi | Art director:
  Emma Campion | Production designers: Mari Gill
  and Faith Hague
Production manager: Dan Myers
Prop stylist: Claire Mack
Copyeditor: Nancy Bailey | Proofreader: Kathy Brock
  | Indexer: Amy Hall
Publicist: Kristin Casemore | Marketer: Chloe Aryeh

10 9 8 7 6 5 4 3 2 1

First Edition